SELECTED
TO
SERVE

SELECTED
TO
SERVE

A Guide for Church Officers

EARL S. JOHNSON, JR.

Geneva Press
Louisville, Kentucky

Scripture quotations, unless otherwise indicated,
are from the New Revised Standard Version
of the Bible, copyright © 1989
by the Division of Christian Education of the National Council
of the Churches of Christ in the U.S.A.,
and are used by permission.

Book design by Sharon Adams
Cover design by Night & Day Design

First edition
Published by Geneva Press
Louisville, Kentucky

This book is printed on acid-free paper that meets the
American National Standards Institute Z39.48 standard. ♾

PRINTED IN THE UNITED STATES OF AMERICA
08 09 — 10 9

Library of Congress Cataloging-in-Publication Data

Johnson, Earl S.
    Selected to serve : a guide for church officers / Earl S. Johnson, Jr.
       p. cm.
    Includes bibliographical references and index.
    ISBN-13: 978-0-664-50165-5 (pbk. : alk. paper)
    ISBN-10: 0-664-50165-6 (pbk. : alk. paper)
        1. Presbyterian Church (U.S.A.)—Church Officers—Handbooks, manuals,
etc. 2. Presbyterian Church (U.S.A.)—Government—Handbooks, manuals, etc.

BX9195 .J64 2000
254'.05137—dc21   00-32766

To my wife, Barbara,
whose love and encouragement
made it possible for me to write this book

Contents

viii **Contents**

Preface

I first learned what it means to be a church officer at the dinner table when I was a boy. My mother and father are both ordained elders in the Presbyterian Church (U.S.A.); they both sang in the choir at First Presbyterian Church, Williamson, New York, and taught church school; at different times they both served on church nominating committees and the pastor nominating committee. They were elected as representatives to presbytery, and my mother made the motion to approve my ordination when it came before Geneva Presbytery. In our house the position of church officer was always held in honor and was considered worthy of respect.

Not much has changed at the table. My wife, Barbara, and I have served four different congregations together, and since she is an ordained elder and deacon, active in Presbyterian Women, has served as a church school teacher, Logos Board member and a regular participant in Church Women United, we still digest the church's news every evening. My thanks to her for helping me understand what it means to be a church officer from the inside out, and for encouraging me to propose this book to Geneva Press in the first place.

Thanks are also due to students at Colgate Rochester Divinity School who participated in my classes on *Presbyterian Polity* and *Confessions in the Presbyterian Tradition* between 1990 and 1998. I learned a great deal from them as we shared experiences and struggled with questions about the true nature of the church together, not only in the classroom, but in the chapel and the refectory as well.

The book you are about to read is designed to help church officers as they learn and share together, especially those who are serving for the first time. It is also written with church officer training sessions for congregations and presbyteries in mind, and I hope it will benefit Presbyterian seminary students who are preparing for their ordination exams or are getting ready to work with their first church. Experienced pastors and church officers may also find it helpful as they struggle with the challenges they face as leaders of the body of Christ.

Much of what appears here has been in print before. Since 1992 I have been privileged to write a column for *Presbyterian Outlook* called "For Church Officers," and I thank the editor, Dr. Robert Bullock, for letting me write about any subject that I considered to be important and valuable. Thanks to him as well for the many dialogues and debates we have enjoyed in person or by phone and e-mail, and for giving permission to reprint any and all materials already published.

I also want to express thanks to Dr. Thomas Long, director of Geneva Press, for his cheerful encouragement and excellent advice about format, style, and outline. Carl Helmich, project editor, and Paul Sumner, copyeditor, both provided careful attention to manuscript details. Their excellent suggestions improved the quality and accuracy of the whole book.

My primary purpose in writing has not been to answer the questions about *how* we work as church leaders, since the *Book of Order* and a number of other books and manuals tell us that, but to consider *why* and *what*. *Why* do we do the things we do as Presbyterians? *What* are the biblical and theological principles behind our decisions? *What* difference will it make if we continue to follow New Testament and Reformed traditions in the future?

As we enter the twenty-first century we face tremendous challenges. There are questions about biblical authority and about who should be allowed to be church officers. We will need courage to work for justice and peace in an increasingly violent world; we will need to see ourselves as parts of a global economy and an ecumenical and interfaith world, spreading the good news in a wired and webbed world. All of these things will challenge our ability to embrace the traditions that made us what we are, while attempting to move faithfully and creatively into a new century that is experiencing changes in culture and technology at blinding speed. May we find ways to straddle the centuries as we learn what it means to follow the Jesus Christ known to believers in the past, while moving into a future that is only beginning to reveal its contours.

Earl S. Johnson, Jr.

The following abbreviations are used for parts of the *Constitution of the Presbyterian Church (U.S.A.)*: C = *Book of Confessions;* G = Form of Government; W = Directory for Worship; D = Rules of Discipline (the last three being sections in the *Book of Order*).

Chapter 1

Being a Church Officer

The Call to Serve

*T*he call of God is to all believers (Rom. 1:6–7; Gal. 1:6; 1 Thess. 2:12; 1 Peter 2:9–10; Jude 1). God calls us individually and as members of the church, and Christians know that when it comes to believing and serving we are not so much the choosers as we are the chosen (John 15:16). Even though we will to believe, there is a surprising and almost inexplicable aspect of Christian vocation which causes us to acknowledge an invisible power of the Spirit that works in our lives long before we make our own conscious decisions (Gal. 1:15; Jer. 1:5; Isa. 49:1; 1 Sam. 1:22, 28).

In addition to the general call to all believers, God also gives unique gifts to individual people to enable them to serve the church in special ways. In the Presbyterian Church (U.S.A.) we recognize some of these gifts by ordaining members as pastors, elders, and deacons. As the *Book of Order* puts it (G-6.0105), "When women and men, by God's providence and gracious gifts, are called by the church to undertake particular forms of ministry, the church shall help them to interpret their call and to be sensitive to the judgments and needs of others." (Also see G-6.0106.)

The history of God's revelation in the Bible indicates that women and men of faith have long been given a special intuition or feeling that leads and sometimes compels them to want to serve. Thus Abraham and Sarah leave a comfortable lifestyle and location to serve God in new ways and in a new place (Gen. 12:1–3; 17:15–16; Heb. 11:8); Moses is directed to set his people free without knowing exactly who sends him (Exodus 3); Ruth feels the divine pull to the God of her mother-in-law (Ruth 1:16); young Samuel hears God's voice in the night (1 Sam. 3:2–14); Jeremiah and Isaiah sense that they are compelled to speak God's word (Jer. 1:9; Isaiah 6). Mary readily accepts the Spirit's call (Luke 1:46–56).

In the New Testament the Greek verb *kaleō* is often used to describe the way believers are called to serve. Paul repeatedly indicates that he is an apostle and qualified to write to churches only because God has summoned him to do so (Rom. 1:1; 1 Cor. 1:1; Gal. 1:1, 15). In Mark 3:13–15 when Jesus called the twelve disciples, "those whom he desired," he gave them three special assignments: to preach the gospel, to heal the sick, and to be with him.

The call of Jesus is particularly important for Christians committed to serving God in the twenty-first century. The church is entering into an unprecedented era of unpredictable change. Pastors and church officers will need to be extremely flexible if churches are going to grow and meet the needs of modern men, women, and children. When we look at Jesus' call, we notice that two of the assignments he gave to his disciples are task oriented. They had to do things: proclaim the good news (evangelize) and serve those who are ill (alleviate suffering, love the poor, and stand up against oppression and prejudice). Yet the third role of those who follow Jesus is one we too often overlook: it calls us simply to be with Jesus and stay close to him. "And he appointed twelve, whom he also named apostles, to be with him" (Mark 3:14).

In the coming years all three assignments will be difficult, but the final one may be the most dangerous and exciting. Being with Jesus means that we have to be so close to him that we know where he is going. Being with Jesus means that we must anticipate where he will be next and meet him there. Being with

Jesus means that we must be willing to take great risks when we know that it is Jesus, and no one else, who is calling us to a particular place and time.

In the Presbyterian Church the call of God is a twofold communication. The first part comes from God through Jesus Christ; the second is issued by a nominating committee of the church and validated by a congregation and/or presbytery (G-1.0306, 14.0100, .0205, .0401; also see 9.0800). In our denomination both elements of the call are necessary for it to be considered genuine. The call to Presbyterian ministry is not a mystical experience amenable only to private review. People cannot claim that God spoke to them in a dream, in the wind, or even in prayer and expect to be ordained solely on that basis.

As Presbyterians we believe that if a call to ordination cannot be perceived and endorsed by the whole body of Christ, it does not exist. Those who serve on the session when members are thinking of becoming inquirers (G-14.0306), or on a presbytery "Preparation for Ministry Committee" (G-14.0300), should not be afraid to give their honest opinions when men and women indicate an interest in becoming church officers or pastors.

When people are truly called to serve God and the body recognizes it, a moment for celebration has been reached. But candidates who are really not qualified to serve because they are spiritually immature, theologically ill fitted, emotionally or psychologically unsuitable, or ill prepared educationally, should be told so plainly by those called by the church to weigh such things, in order to save them pain, the illusion of false expectations, and the expense of pursuing a vocation or position they are not qualified to hold in the first place. The Preparation for Ministry Committee of presbytery has to work prayerfully, sensitively, and confidentially with sessions when those requesting the status of an inquirer are not qualified to take this step.

Elders have a similar responsibility when the congregational nominating committee is ready to invite members to become elders or deacons (or trustees). According to our constitution, the session is "to instruct, examine, ordain, install, and welcome into common ministry elders and deacons on their election by the congregation and to inquire into their faithfulness in fulfilling their responsibilities" (G-10.0102l). While a call must always be open to all members (it cannot be denied on the basis of sex, racial or ethnic background, or economic status), the session does have the right to examine those whom the nominating committee selects. This duty is an important and solemn one. As Joan S. Gray and Joyce C. Tucker indicate, it is the responsibility of the session to determine if each person elected to office has the essential knowledge to serve in a Presbyterian church, and to inquire about her or his personal faith and understanding of the office. If the session does not approve the nomination of such candidates, it will report its findings to the nominating committee and call a special congregational meeting to fill resulting vacancies (G-14.0205).[1] In such a sensitive situation, those who have not been allowed to proceed to ordination will need the pastoral care and love of the pastor and the members of the church to avoid ongoing hurt feelings and disappointment.

A call to ministry is always one that must be considered carefully and be taken seriously. Those who are thinking about the possibility of becoming pastors often ask how they will know for certain that God really wants them to make such a vocational change. Many times the radical choice to enter full-time pastoral ministry will make a big difference in their lives: they may have to leave a lucrative job, apply for loans to attend theological seminary, disrupt family life by giving up a comfortable income, or force spouses and children to move to a new area. Following God's call may mean real sacrifice for everyone involved. Yet there is at least one answer to the question "How do I know I am called?" It is this: "When you can no longer do anything else, then you will know that God has definitely called you."

Sometimes God's choice is easy to see and skills and gifts obviously fit people to serve the church. On other occasions the voice of God through the church is a surprise. Members and pastors frequently wonder why a nominating committee has recommended an individual for a position of responsibility, only to learn later that this person has just the talents needed in a difficult or sensitive situation that could never have been anticipated. In one church where I served, I was not entirely pleased when the nominating committee selected four business people to fill all the vacancies on the session. It did not seem to me that the selection was broad enough to represent the whole congregation. Nevertheless, after they were elected and ordained we discovered why God called them to serve. During the next year the nation suffered through a severe economic downturn, and when we had to make drastic adjustments to church spending, the four business leaders were not in the least concerned. "You do not need to worry," they said, almost in one voice. "We know how to take care of it." And they did.

Questions for Study

1. *What are some of the similarities and some of the differences of the biblical call stories? (See Gen. 12:1–3; 17:15–16; Ruth 1:16; 1 Sam. 3:2–14; Jer. 1:1–10; Isaiah 6; Mark 3:13–19; Acts 9:1–20; 22:6–16; 26:9–18.)*

2. *Do you think God calls men and women in similar ways today?*

3. *How do people "hear" the call today? How do they know it is more than mere wish fulfillment?*

4. *How important is it to have a call validated by the church in order to enter into ministry?*

Elders

The position of elder is the oldest active office still being used in the Christian church today. Although the apostleship no doubt precedes it in prestige, power, and antiquity, it did not remain a permanent office since it was limited to those who had a direct commission from the risen Jesus himself and had unique gifts from the Holy Spirit (Acts 1:1–26; 1 Cor. 12:1–11, 29). Paul indicates that he became an apostle sometime after the original apostles were commissioned and hints that he may have been the last person in the church to hold that title (1 Cor. 15:8–10).

The New Testament tells us that when the apostles planted churches they appointed elders to govern the congregations in their absence (Acts 14:23; Titus 1:5; see also Acts 20:17; 2 John 1; 3 John 1). The Greek word for elder is *presbyteros*—literally, "an older person," "a wise person," "a leader." It is the basis of the name of our church and its form of government. In the Old Testament an elder was one of a group of wise men who were elected or appointed to rule a city. The term is used in the New Testament as a title for Jewish leaders (see Matt. 15:2; 16:21; Mark 7:3, 5; Acts 4:5, 8, 23; 6:12; Heb. 11:2). Recently archaeologists have discovered benches outside excavated city gates in Israel where elders actually sat and made their rulings.

Although it is not certain what the elders' responsibilities were in the early church, their position was clearly one of honor. First Timothy (5:17–22 and 6:3–19) indicates that they were worthy of being paid and were expected to exhibit the highest moral character. Elders were to be compassionate, humble, and eager to serve the congregation like a shepherd, following the example of Christ (1 Peter 5:1–10). They were often engaged in a healing ministry (James 5:13–18).

In the Presbyterian Church there have traditionally been two kinds of presbyters: the teaching elders or pastors, and the lay elders, who are elected members of sessions. Together, through shared powers and divided responsibilities they govern the church. According to the "Historic Principles of Church Government" adopted by the General Assembly in 1797 (G-1.0400), the Presbyterian Church is a democratic one in which the representatives of the whole govern every part of the church, the majority rules, and decisions (based on "the collected wisdom and united voice of the whole Church") are founded on the example of the apostles and the practice of the early church.

The responsibilities of lay people elected as elders are clearly laid out in the *Book of Order* (G-6.0300, 10.0000ff., and 14.0200ff.). They include the encouragement of the congregation in the worship of God, the equipping of the church in mission in the world, the comfort and care of the sick with special attention to the poor and the oppressed, and service in the higher governing bodies of the church. In the local church, the session—with the exception of certain rights and privileges granted to the congregation and pastors—has virtual oversight of all the spiritual, educational, and practical activities of the church. As Presbyterians we believe that the Holy Spirit works best in our church through the will of the people as represented by its elders, rather than in a top-down fashion through the command of a priest or pastor or through the direction of an executive presbyter, superintendent, or bishop. Even though the elders are given a great deal of power, a heavy responsibility is also laid on them. Elders must not be power hungry, petty, or vindictive but must be spiritually wise, committed primarily to following Jesus Christ as his servants, and of high moral character (G-6.0106, .0303). The session is not a training ground for new members or new Christians, for gossips or people who want to control others; elders must be those who are spiritually and psychologically mature and are more concerned for the health of the church and the work of God's kingdom than they are for their own positions or reputations. Elders must be men and women who are not only committed to Presbyterian principles of government; they must also be those who are constantly open to change and the fresh breezes of the Holy Spirit which give the church vitality and new opportunities to do God's work.

Questions for Study

1. *What kind of personal and spiritual characteristics do you think members should have before they are chosen to be elders?*
2. *Is the office of elder respected in your congregation?*
3. *Is the session truly representative in your congregation?*
4. *Do you think that the position of elder is as important as that of an ordained pastor?*

Deacons

Our title of deacon comes from a word with roots in Greek history, *diakoneō*. In its most basic form it can mean "to serve," "to wait on table," "to be a slave."

It is this concept of service that the early church adopted to describe the function of the compassionate, caring arm of Christian mission. At the beginning of the twenty-first century it is hard to imagine that in response to the question "What position in the church is the one with the most prestige?" the answer would be "to be the servant of all," but that is exactly what the first Christians believed. In the first century, being a slave was usually a demeaning, humiliating station in life, and today few people choose waiting on tables as a lifetime profession. Where did the New Testament believers get such an image to describe the work of God? The answer is that they obviously got it from Jesus himself.

One of the keystones of Jesus' thinking is that humility and self-giving are two characteristics God requires of the children of the kingdom. Basing his teaching on Old Testament servant passages (Isa. 41:8–20; 42:1–9, 18–22; 53:1–12; 61:1–4; see Luke 4:16–30), he tells his disciples that putting God's work ahead of their own needs and desires is the highest priority (Mark 10:35–45; Matt. 23:11; John 12:24–26).

The earliest reference in the New Testament to the office of deacon is found in Paul's letter to the Philippians (1:1). Here Paul greets all the saints in Christ Jesus who are in Philippi, along with the bishops and deacons. At this time there seems to have been little distinction between the positions of bishop and deacon, and they differed in function rather than rank.

In a letter written later by one of Paul's disciples, they are linked again, in 1 Timothy 3:1–13, where the spiritual and moral requirements of both offices are listed. A bishop must be above reproach, sensible, dignified, temperate, and a good manager of his own household. Likewise deacons must be serious, not drunkards or greedy, and understand the mystery of the faith. Verse 11 may well indicate that women were already called to be deacons at this early date, just as Romans 16:1 lists Phoebe as one of the deacons in the church at Cenchreae, and Junia is called an apostle (Rom. 16:6).

More specific information about the origin of the office of deacon is found in Acts 6:1–7. Here Luke describes how Greek-speaking Christians complained to the Hebrew-speaking leaders of the Jerusalem church that their widows were being neglected in the daily distribution of food and money. As a result, it was decided that seven people should be selected to carry out the caring and serving work of the church by waiting on table at the church's "love feasts" and taking care of the poor. Meanwhile the apostles would continue a ministry of preaching and prayer. That the office of deacon quickly matured is indicated by the fact that Stephen was not martyred for being a waiter but for proclaiming God's word.

In the *Book of Order* (G-6.0400–.0407) the description of the functions of deacons in the Presbyterian Church is clearly based on these New Testament precedents. "The office of deacon as set forth in Scripture is one of sympathy, witness, and service after the example of Jesus Christ." It is the duty of deacons to minister to those who are in need, to the sick and friendless and any who are in distress. In many congregations each deacon is assigned families to contact and minister to on a regular basis. In other churches, programs such as the Stephen Ministry are adopted to shoulder some of the caring. It is also possible for deacons to assume other functions such as administering programs for the elderly or working with the handicapped or those economically deprived. In some parts of the country the board of deacons also monitors the finances of the church.

Deacons perform a very necessary function in the Presbyterian Church and represent the heart of what it means to be a Christian. We can all be like deacons, of course, whether we hold ordained office or not, since whenever we reach out in love to those in need, we reach out in the name and love of Christ himself and are following his example of serving the hungry and thirsty (Matt. 25:35–46).

Questions for Study

1. *Why did the early church first create the ministry of deacons (Acts 6:1–7)?*
2. *What does it mean to call the deacons "the caring arm of the church"?*
3. *How many functions do the deacons perform in your church?*
4. *Do you know of people in your church who do the work of deacons but are not ordained?*

Pastors

After the death and resurrection of Jesus the early church had four major offices (apostles, elders, deacons, and bishops), which differed in function rather than rank. Other positions included those of prophets, evangelists, teachers (Eph. 4:11), administrators, and healers (1 Cor. 12:27–30).[2]

Although it is not precisely certain what people did when they held these positions, we can see that many of their functions have been assumed in the modern office of pastor or minister. The *Book of Order* specifically states (G-6.0200ff.) that Presbyterian pastors are responsible for the ministry of the Word and Sacrament, for studying, teaching, and preaching the Word, for encouraging the people in worship and prayer, for equipping them for their tasks, for exercising pastoral care for the sick, poor, troubled, and dying, and for participating actively in the ministry of the church in governing bodies above the session level.

Not all ministers are pastors in local churches. Men and women may be ordained as teachers, professors, chaplains, pastoral counselors, campus ministers, evangelists, administrators, social workers, and professionals in other institutions. Some clergy who have secular vocations may also serve as parish associates or temporary supplies (G-14.0515, .0513). Pastors are not members of the local church but are members of the presbytery in the region in which they reside.

In many ways the role of pastor in a church today is terribly demanding, and it is nearly impossible for one person to fulfill all the expectations of church members. In a booklet designed to help sessions evaluate pastoral performance, a list of twenty-two functions is given, ranging from corporate worship leadership to professional growth.[3] Today the list would no doubt be even longer. Pastors need the prayers and support of their congregations as they try to satisfy the widely diverse expectations that they be preachers, human resource directors, administrators, teachers, fund raisers, counselors, crisis managers, planners, community leaders, television personalities, webmasters, and presbyters. More than ever, pastors need to be men and women of great integrity, of spiritual depth, solid education, stable maturity, and careful flexibility as the church enters into the changing and challenging environment of the twenty-first century.

The New Testament provides one image of the pastor that helps the church keep pastoral duties in perspective. In John 21:15–19 the risen Jesus urges Peter and the other disciples to remember that their chief function is to feed God's sheep. One of the Greek words behind our term "pastor" is *poimēn,* "shepherd" (Eph. 4:11), and it comes to the church directly out of Jesus' own teaching that he was himself "the good shepherd" (John 10:14, 16; see Heb. 13:20), the one who compassionately teaches, feeds, and guards his sheep (Mark 6:34). The author of 1 Peter 5 expands this image and advises certain elders "to tend the flock of God that is in your charge," to do so eagerly and not under compulsion, and to serve with humility as examples to the flock. If pastors and church members can remember that a pastor is not expected to be perfect or to be all things to all people, but is only required to work with and love his or her people and be faithful to God's calling in Christ, we all might have a better vision of what pastoral ministry really is and could be.

Questions for Study

1. *What are the most important qualifications of a pastor?*
2. *What can a pastor do in the Presbyterian Church that no one else can do?*
3. *Do you think the job of a pastor is easy or difficult? How can members of the church support their pastors?*

Trustees

An office in the Presbyterian Church which does not trace its roots back to New Testament but is nevertheless equally important in our denomination today is that of trustee.

In colonial days Presbyterians were obligated to appoint trustees because their churches were not maintained by the British or Colonial governments as established churches. Private individuals had to have church property conveyed to them, and they took legal responsibility for it so that the churches could keep what they had.[4] Later, when the United States was formed and permitted churches to hold and manage property, the position of trustee was changed to meet incorporation requirements of various states.[5] In our present polity, churches can have trustees function in one of two ways: if the trustees and the session form two separate units the boards are said to be *bicameral;* if all of the elders are trustees and the session does the work of the trustees, it is *unicameral.*

According to the *Book of Order,* trustees are to be elected by the congregation at the recommendation of the nominating committee (G-7.0400–.0403) and have the power to receive, hold, encumber, manage, and transfer real or personal property for the church, to accept and execute deeds of title to such property, and to hold and defend property titles—all subject to the provisions of the *Constitution* and the will of the session, congregation, and presbytery.

In many churches, trustees are given responsibility to maintain church buildings and lands, manage the church budget, provide suitable insurance coverage, invest capital, and do long-range financial planning. If the trustees comprise a separate board they are always responsible to the session and its oversight and direction. If the church has a unicameral board the session constitutes special committees to undertake trustee functions. Whichever board functions as trustees, it needs to be understood that all property managed by the local church is not technically owned by that church. As the *Book of Order* points out (G-8.0100–.0700), all property held by or for a particular church, presbytery, or synod or the General Assembly is held in trust for the use and benefit of the Presbyterian Church (U.S.A.) as a whole and is not the exclusive possession of the governing body that manages it. Although this part of our government is often misunderstood, it makes good sense. Since Presbyterian churches were founded in accordance with accepted principles of the Reformed tradition, it would not be right to allow a church to be easily turned into a sanctuary housing a congregation with views antithetical to the Presbyterian *Constitution,* or a bowling alley, or the meeting place of a group fomenting violence and murder. Although at the time of reunion in 1983 the possibility of exemption was granted for PCUS churches that might have incorporated under different laws, such an exemption expired June 10, 1991, and is no longer valid (G-8.0701; *Articles of Agreement* 13.1–.4).

Occasionally church members mistakenly assume that trustees are responsible for the practical matters of the church, whereas the session should concern itself only with spiritual issues. Such a misunderstanding almost always leads to rivalry and fracture within the congregation. Trustees do deal with everyday issues, but only under the direction of the session, and there is virtually no part of church life that is not the session's responsibility. What is more, it is incorrect to imagine that trustees do not need to have the spiritual concerns of the church in mind. Trustees must be men and women of spiritual wisdom and power, persons who are deeply committed to Jesus Christ and the mission of the Presbyterian Church (U.S.A.) and who understand and support the overall program of the church.

In most churches that have two boards the issue of authority never needs to be raised. If the trustees and session keep in constant communication, if each sends representatives to the meetings of the other board, and if the pastor acts as a coordinator of activities, the two can work as true parts of the body of Christ, almost like two hands of the same church, always with Christ as the head.

At a time when the management of church finances is extremely difficult and the maintenance of property is very time-consuming and costly, at a time when investments can be changed instantly over the Internet, the Presbyterian Church is blessed to have so many women and men with practical and professional experience who can be called upon to benefit our congregations and higher governing bodies. As good stewards of the church's property and endowments, they serve an important role in preserving the assets of the church of Christ for future generations.

Questions for Study

1. *In what sense do the trustees perform a spiritual office?*
2. *What kind of people should serve on a board of trustees? What kind of talents and experience should they have in your particular church?*
3. *Should trustees be interested in the mission of the church or just the "nuts and bolts"?*

Deciding That a Call Has Changed: Grapefruit Theology

Those of us who are already serving the church need to remember that God can surprise us with a new calling. Even though the call of an ordained officer is normally for life in the Presbyterian Church (G-14.0203), we must all be open to the winds of the Spirit and look for new experiences and fresh opportunities, recognizing that the one who gave us our gifts in the first place may know that our experiences and talents have prepared us for entirely new endeavors. If such a thing happens, it is our responsibility to listen once more to God's voice and be ready to go wherever we are led, prepared to demonstrate again that, along with Paul, we believe that the God who called us into the fellowship of the Son is faithful and will sustain us to the end (1 Cor. 1:9).

These kinds of changes are always difficult. Very few of us are able to make them gracefully, with style and ease. Yet change comes in our calling, in our churches, at home, at work, and in our private lives, whether we like it or are ready or not. Often we cannot avoid these changes; always we cannot completely control them.

One metaphor that may help Christians understand and deal with changes in call could be called "Grapefruit Theology." Like all metaphors, it has its limitations. If you push it too far, it falls apart; but it can help us perceive how God works when life is not what we expect.

Think of the church or of life as a grapefruit. It is a whole, an integrated sphere. Yet your life and your ability to make decisions is only one segment of that grapefruit. God expects you to be part of the whole by being faithful in your part. Although you know you are part of the grapefruit, you are not responsible for what happens in the next segment or in a segment on another part of the grapefruit. Not only are you not responsible, but God will not allow you to be. What God expects is for you to be faithful where you are.

If, for example, the pastor accepts a call to a new church, he or she has to make the decision based on what God is calling him or her to do. (The discussion here is about a call, not long-range planning.) If other members of the staff are also considering a change and they cannot share that information because of matters of confidentiality, their responsibility also is to listen to God's voice in their lives and act upon it. The rub is that it is incumbent on all parties to follow God's will, even though none of them can see the whole. God is in control and coordinates the final outcome. If I am faithful in my part, and the others are faithful in theirs, God's plan is fulfilled. If we are not faithful, then it is possible that my segment is wrong, and that the whole grapefruit will become rotten, because God's plan for the part—and consequently for the whole—is disrupted. From a human perspective, the changes may seem confusing and uncoordinated. But from God's point of view the mission of the church may be proceeding exactly as planned.

The difficulty of proceeding with changes in ministry despite a grasp of the total picture is what Oswald Chambers calls "the bewildering call of God."[6] His language is not inclusive and is quoted exactly.

> The call of God can never be understood absolutely or explained externally; it is a call that can only be perceived and understood internally by our inner-nature. The call of God is like the call of the sea—no one hears it except the person who has the nature of the sea in him. What God calls us to do cannot be definitely stated, because His call is simply to be His friend and to accomplish His own purposes. Our real test is in truly believing that God knows what He desires.

If we can understand how God's call works in segments and in the whole, and trust in the knowledge and wisdom of God, we can move to a simplicity and calm that is, as Chambers puts it, "characteristic of the children of God." As God said to Joshua, "Be strong and courageous; do not be frightened or dismayed, for the Lord is with you wherever you go" (Josh. 1:9).

Questions for Study

1. *Study Paul's change in calling from a Pharisee to a Christian leader in Acts 9. Do you think that Presbyterians are called by God in such a dramatic fashion today?*

2. *How would a pastor know when it is time to change churches? How does God let a church officer know that he or she has something different to do in the church or in a secular vocation?*

When Should a Church Officer Resign?

Most members of a church have experienced the departure of a pastor. It happens in the life of all congregations periodically: whenever the pastor believes that God is issuing a call to a new church or another job; whenever there is a mismatch between expectations and talents; when retirement finally comes. Fortunately there is a good bit of help available when this decision needs to be made. Excellent materials can assist pastors and congregations when they decide that a change is necessary.[7] The *Book of Order* provides the proper procedure for the dissolution of a pastoral relationship (G-14.0600), and the General Assembly provides detailed steps to the presbytery's Committee on Ministry to help congregations make an orderly transition.

Unfortunately, similar guidelines are not available for the resignation of church officers. Although it is usually assumed that an elder, deacon, or trustee will normally serve out a three-year term, that is not always in the best interest of the church or the individual. Even when it is obvious that an officer should leave the session or a board, there is no clear mechanism to enable the departure, short of disciplinary action (D-10.0100–14.0502) or the renunciation of jurisdiction by the officer (G-6.0500). In most churches, moreover, other officers and church members are reluctant to discuss the problem openly, fearing the painful conflict and hurt feelings that may erupt. Sometimes church members try to force out a church officer or pastor through subterranean means: snubbing the person in question, refusing to increase a pastor's salary, complaining secretly to the Committee on Ministry, etc. Usually, however, resolution by avoidance or subterfuge is not the best way to proceed. Openness and direct action are healthier for the church and the individuals involved.

If you are a church officer, how do you know when it is time to resign?

1. Certainly it is time to leave the session, board of deacons, or board of trustees if health problems or major changes in your

job or family make it difficult or impossible for you to participate actively (G-14.0210). If your continuing absence leaves a real gap, your friends and fellow church members must do the work you should be doing.

2. It might also be time to resign if changes in your lifestyle, your ethical code, or your beliefs put you in direct conflict with one or more of the vows you took when you were ordained or installed (see the discussion in chapter 7 below), or with the high standards our constitution demands of church officers (see chapter 8), or if actions of the church violate your conscience (G-1.0301).

3. An officer might also consider resignation if he or she feels out of sync with the church most of the time. Although it sometimes seems commendable to "hang in there," "tough it out," or "fight the good fight," nothing very positive is accomplished by the church member who holds on simply because "this is my church, always has been, always will be." If you find yourself losing sleep over session decisions; if you are angry at the pastor all the time and have taken upon yourself the task of keeping him or her on track; if you feel it is your duty to protect the church against some real or imagined danger; if you find yourself plotting more and worshiping less; or if you constantly have a knot in your stomach whenever you go into the church building, then it is probably best for your own spiritual health and for the future of the church to step aside and let someone else shoulder your responsibilities.

4. It may also be time to leave if you find—after discussion with church friends, honest analysis of your own feelings, and careful prayer—that your opposition to church actions, to the pastor, or to another officer is not based on Christian commitment or God's will but is based on deep-rooted resentment, a desire to get even, a personality conflict, or raw power politics. Every church officer takes a vow to further the peace, unity, and purity of the church (G-14.0207g). But if we discover that we are more a part of the problem than the solution, then it may be time, with an attitude of honesty, humility, and forgiveness, to move along.

Although churches like to hide painful conditions, officers

find themselves in difficult situations often enough to know it is better to face them honesty and openly, before they cause division and discord within the church that might take many years to heal. As pastors and church officers, we all have desires for power, feelings that get hurt, and egos that can get in the way of our calling. When we find that we are no longer serving Jesus Christ in joy and love, it may be time to remove ourselves from the conflicted situation and, if necessary, even find a new church where we are more comfortable within ourselves and where our gifts are better appreciated and more useful to God.

Questions for Study

1. *Do you know anyone who has resigned an ordained position?*
2. *Do you know anyone who should resign?*
3. *Elders and deacons are permitted to serve two three-year terms. Do you think it is beneficial and wise for an officer to serve for six years?*
4. *How do pastors and churches know when a pastoral ministry should end?*

Keep the Faith, Baby!

Being a Presbyterian officer can be a very exciting and challenging opportunity. For many people, God has used the experience to change their lives dramatically as they have taken on new responsibilities, met new people, and learned how the church really works. For new elders, deacons, and pastors, the ordination service can be a very moving experience as they sense the power and exhilaration of God's call. Frequently they are nearly overwhelmed with the seriousness of their task when they are asked, "Will you seek to serve the people with energy, intelligence, imagination, and love?" (G-14.0405).

Nevertheless, one does not have to be on a church board for many months or serve as pastor for a long time before difficult circumstances create discouragement and anxiety. Serving the church is hard, demanding work, and it is not without reason that Jesus promises his followers that one thing they can be sure of as disciples is persecution and suffering (Mark 13:9–13). Elders, deacons, trustees, and pastors must work hard to create a team atmosphere, a synergistic fellowship, where everyone wins and everyone works for the whole. Church officers with experience know that problems abound in running a church, that there will always be critics and that nothing worth doing comes easily.

One way to avoid the discouragement that routinely plagues the governing of a church is to make sure officers are carefully trained before they assume responsibility. Nothing is more frustrating than serving on a board or committee without being told what the expectations are, what the tasks involve, and what the protocols include. Many presbyteries offer officer training classes for the whole presbytery or in regional clusters. If presbytery-wide training sessions are not available, a local church can easily set up its own class to prepare its officers. Elements that might be given in a typical three-hour Saturday morning class include:

> Opening Prayer
> The Nature of Church Office
> > The Call
> > The Excitement
> > The Reality
> > Keeping the Faith
> Discussion of the *Book of Order* and the Role of Governing Bodies
> Review of the *Book of Confessions*
> The Biblical Concept of Ordained Offices
> What Each Board Does in Particular
> Our Church Budget
> Questions
> Final Prayer

It is often helpful to invite pastors and elders from other churches to lead discussion or to ask for assistance from the presbytery's moderator, stated clerk, or executive presbyter. The videotape *Across the Centuries: The Book of Order Today*, by Donald I. MacInnes (Interlink Video Productions, 1990), is a particularly helpful tool on the subject.

One way to have some fun (and learn at the same time) is to develop a questionnaire to help new officers become acquainted with the *Book of Order.* To use the following questions, ask officers to answer them by themselves without any discussion or reference books. Then go over the questions one at a time, with the whole group, looking up answers in the *Book of Order* and discussing further ramifications.

The D.A. (or Devil's Advocate) asks questions or makes challenging statements on these topics.

I. Policy Questions

A. *D.A. to young parents:* "It does not matter that the minister is out of town. Any one of the elders can baptize your baby."

   Response: According to our constitution, who can baptize? (G-6.0202)

B. *D.A. to custodian:* "You are the one who has to clean up this place, so you should decide when the building should be used and by whom."

   Response: Who is accountable for church property? (G-10.0100n)

C. *D.A. to the young adult group:* "Since you are the parents of most of the children in the church school, you can decide when church school and the service of worship takes place. You can even cut out these activities if they conflict with vacation or family plans."

   Response: Who has the authority to decide when and where the service of worship will be held? (G-10.0100d)

D. *D.A. to young couple:* "You do not need to worry about your wedding. The session will approve it since they know your parents."

Response: Who decides whether or not a couple should be married?
(W-4.9000b)

II. Specific Questions from the *Book of Order*

A. How often does the session have to meet?
1. Once a month
2. Quarterly
3. Whenever the pastor feels like it
4. Only when the pastor or two elders call it
(G-10.0200)

B. Who is supposed to visit the pastor annually?
1. The Executive Presbyter
2. The Committee on Ministry
3. The Visiting Committee
4. The Committee on Representation
(G-11.0502)

C. Who draws up the budget of the local church?
1. The Board of Trustees
2. A committee made up of the treasurer, the pastor and the chairperson of the Board of Trustees.
3. A budget committee made up of representatives from the session, trustees, and the deacons
4. None of the above
(G-10.0102i)

III. Questions from *Robert's Rules of Order*

A. To raise a question of privilege means
1. Inquire about one's social status
2. Wonder why the pastor is a member of the country club
3. Ask permission to go to the restroom
4. Make a request that requires immediate attention because of its urgency (§19)

B. Which motions are not debatable?
1. Adopt, accept or agree to a report
2. Adjournment

3. Limit the debate on a pending question
4. Division of the house
5. Dispense with the reading of the minutes
6. All of the above

C. The "order of the day" refers to:
1. The order of worship for a presbytery meeting
2. Sending out for lunch
3. The prayer used that day from the prayer book
4. A subject, question, or item of business set in advance to be taken up at a particular time (§40)

D. An ex-officio member is:
1. A past moderator of the presbytery
2. An unofficial member who can attend but must remain silent
3. An officer of the order of the day
4. A member of the board by virtue of an office who can speak but cannot vote (§48)

Of course, more than training is needed to prevent discouragement. As officers called by God, we need to keep our faith strong through sharing, prayer, routine worship, and Bible study. Prayer is a powerful tool for doing the church's work and constantly reminds us that as members of the body of Christ none of us is expected to do the work of the whole body alone. Each one can do his or her part, but it is only together that we constitute the whole body, with Christ as the Head (1 Cor. 12:4–31). Part of our work is to keep looking ahead to God's future (Heb. 11:1) and to trust that if we have been called, God will empower us through the Spirit to accomplish whatever has been set out for us to do. As Paul says in Philippians 4:13, "I can do all things in [God] who strengthens me."

Questions for Study

1. *How do you keep up your strength in times of trouble in the church?*

2. *Are there any promises in the Bible that help responsible officers keep their faith when times are tough?*

Chapter 2

Questions Officers Often Ask

How Do Officers Get Elected?
The Nominating Committee

According to the *Book of Order* one of the primary responsibilities of the local church is to elect and ordain officers to fulfill particular functions (G-6.0102). The expectations and requirements are high: they should be men and women of strong faith, dedicated discipleship, and should exhibit the love of Jesus Christ in their lives. They are also required to lead a life in obedience to Scripture and in conformity to the historic confessional standards of the church (G-6.0106; see the discussions below in chapters 4, 5, and 6).

But how are officers chosen? The only way members of the church can be called to office is through the nomination of a representative nominating committee elected by the congregation. But how does such a committee get elected and how does it function?

A nominating committee is a prime example of democracy in action in our church and illustrates one of the historic principles of church order—that the power to elect officers who will have authority over a society rests solely in that society (G-1.0306). Although high standards are set by our *Constitution* for the qualifications of the officers, the ultimate right to choose those who will represent them is entirely up to the members of the local church. This concept of government by representation is part of our heritage that goes back to what the General Assembly of the Presbyterian Church in 1797 called "the radical [fundamental] principles of Presbyterian church government and discipline," whereby "a larger part of the Church, or a representation of it, should govern a smaller, or determine matters of controversy which arise therein; that, in like manner, a representation of the whole should govern and determine in regard to every part, and to all the parts united: that is, that a majority shall govern" (G-1.0400).

Part of the responsibility of a congregational nominating committee is to make sure true representation is achieved. The committee itself must meet this standard: to include both men and women, giving fair representation to persons of all age groups, people from different racial and ethnic groups within the congregation, and to those members who have disabilities (G-14.0202). Such requirements are not only just and fair; they also make practical sense. Those who govern the church need to understand that they represent *all* the members; they need to know what the people think, what issues are of major concern, which matters are lightning rods in the history of the church; and they need to know how a particular church works on a day-to-day basis in order to lead wisely and well.

A nominating committee must be composed according to a constitutional pattern: at least two members must be elders selected by the session, and at least one must be a current member of the session who is willing to serve as moderator. One member is designated by and comes from the board of deacons. Other members of the committee shall be selected by the congregation in a manner they choose, but these members must make up the majority. None of the at-large members can be current members of the session or board of deacons. The pastor serves ex officio; he or she can speak but cannot vote (G-14.0201b).

Many congregations develop means by which the nominating committee can represent the whole congregation. In addition to the constitutional requirements already mentioned, efforts are made to ensure that major groups are represented: youth members; single members, people working in Christian education, music and worship, finance, mission and outreach; members of the Board of Trustees, Stephen Ministry, etc.[1]

How does the nominating committee do its work? Certainly one of the key tools is the discipline of prayer. In a real sense, the nominating committee of the congregation is the conduit through which God funnels the call to ministry into the local church. This places an awesome burden on the members of the committee to be so open to the work of the Holy Spirit that they cannot misunderstand God's will. The nominating committee cannot fulfill its responsibilities adequately without asking God for guidance on a regular basis, both as a committee and as individuals participating in their own private prayer life.

To make sure that the nominating committee knows the best candidates for the offices of elder, deacon, or trustee, it should ask the congregation for help. It is best to put a notice in the church bulletin, and send out a letter to the congregation asking for the recommendations of members, well before the committee begins selecting names of people it wants to contact for office. Elements in the letter might include the following:

- An explanation of the work of the committee and its time line
- The constitutional and spiritual requirements for church officers
- Lists of the specific duties for elders, deacons, and trustees
- The names of the current officers, the years of their terms, and the officers whose terms are expiring
- Blank spaces where members can indicate the name, address, and phone number of the people they are suggesting, along with information about previous offices held, experience in church service, and spiritual qualifications that make them good candidates
- Members should also be encouraged to suggest their own names if they feel called to serve.

If the church has a computerized talent bank, the nominating committee will want to look at information the members have given about their own experiences and their willingness to serve on various boards and committees in the future. Often it is helpful to have available copies of a photographic church directory so the committee can see whom they are talking about. Some computer programs allow digital photographs to be attached to vital information about each member.

When the committee has received the input of the congregation it is time to survey the vacancies to be filled. Church records need to be consulted to determine which officers will be ineligible to serve another term. Church officers can be elected to three-year terms, but they cannot serve consecutive terms which total more than six years of service. Reelection is not possible until a year has passed (G-14.0201). Those who have served a single term should be asked if they want to serve another three years (if that is the will of the nominating committee). Although most officers are renominated, it is possible that the committee will not want to ask a person to serve a second term if his or her activity on a board has been ineffective, inappropriate, or unethical.

Other caveats: (1) The church should not use the positions of elder, deacon, and trustee to break in new members, give people experience, or try to encourage members to become active again. Being on a church board requires spiritual wisdom, experience, commitment, and a proven willingness to work hard on the church's behalf. There are other committees and groups in the church that can serve as training grounds for potential officers. (2) It is also unwise to ask close members of the same family to serve on the same board (husbands and wives, mothers and sons, etc.), since it creates the appearance of nepotism and can, in fact, give one family an inappropriate amount of power.

As the committee prepares to select members to contact about filling vacancies on various boards, some process needs to be set up that will ensure there is no confusion about the order in which calls or contacts are made. Usually one member of the committee is asked to work on filling one vacancy. Elder Jones might be asked to call Miss Smith to fill in Elder Vacancy No. 1, If Miss Smith declines, then Mr. Jones calls the committee chairperson to get another name from the prioritized list. The chairperson serves as clearing house (perhaps with a laptop computer near the telephone) to make sure no one is assigned to fill two vacancies or that two people are put in the same slot.

In most cases the best way to ask people to serve as church officers is face to face. A phone call setting up an appointment to discuss the committee's request could be enhanced by a short script that enables committee members to say more or less the same thing every time they call someone. Meeting with candidates in person gives them more time to ask questions and find out exactly what is expected of them. They may want to know who already serves on the committee, how many meetings there are per month, and when they take place. Candidates may want to pray about the decision, talk to a spouse or friend, or call current members of the board to find out what they think before making a final decision.

Often, of course, there is not time to set up personal visits, and they may be unnecessary if the candidate has previously served in the office. In such cases, it is still important to take enough time to explain what is expected and make sure the person being asked to serve understands the requirements of the office.

Under normal conditions, officers are elected at the annual meeting of the congregation (G-14.0204, 7.0302).[2] Usually the slate of officers is printed in the report distributed to the members beforehand, and the moderator invites the chairperson of the nominating committee to make a motion for each office being filled. Nominations are invited from the floor, and if there is more than one candidate per office, voting is done by secret ballot. It is a good idea to have paper ballots ready if such a need arises. A majority of the members present are needed to elect the new officers.[3]

Questions for Study

1. *If you were going to list three top qualifications for each of the elected offices in the church, what would they be?*
2. *What kind of people should serve on the nominating committee?*
3. *Would you like to have more than one nominee for each office and allow candidates to run against each other for church office?*

What Are the Duties of Church Officers?

Elders are elected to serve on the session for three-year terms, with the possibility of reelection to a second term, provided that the time of service does not exceed six years. The title of elder is retained even when a man or woman is no longer serving on the session. Therefore it is possible for one congregation to have many elders in the church, including those who were ordained in other congregations within the Presbyterian Church (U.S.A.).

Since the session is the ruling body of the church, and because it is responsible for most of the decisions and policies that are made, members of the session are asked to perform a wide range of activities (G-10.0000). Elders on the session may make numerous decisions, such as: to direct the evangelism program of the church, receive or transfer members, lead the congregation in mission, direct the circumstances of worship, provide for church growth, develop and supervise the church school, develop principles and programs of stewardship, establish and finalize the church budget, lead the church in its mission to the world, instruct, examine, ordain, and install new elders and deacons, direct the employment policies of the church, provide for the management of the church, maintain relationships with higher governing bodies of the church and churches in other denominations, and keep an accurate roll of the membership of the church.

Because one person cannot be responsible for the details of so many activities, the session is usually divided into committees. In many churches they include Mission and Outreach, Christian Education, Worship and Music, Finance, Buildings and Grounds, Membership and Evangelism, Personnel, and Endowments. Larger congregations often have additional committees, which may include Youth, Adult Education, Church Growth, Capital Improvement, Interpretation and Stewardship, Communication (for the development and implementation of policies about church advertising in newspapers, television, etc., and the utilization of the Internet and e-mail), and others. Members are generally asked to serve on at least one of the session's committees and need to plan their monthly schedule accordingly.

Elders can also serve on committees and boards on a presbytery, synod, or General Assembly level. Since each session elects representatives as commissioners to the presbytery, some elders may attend regular presbytery meetings as well as committee functions in their own church.

In addition to these activities, session members are usually expected to remain active in the life of the congregation, attending special worship events, extra meetings of the session and congregation, receptions for new and departing members, long-range planning sessions, and so forth. Elders are also called upon to lead the congregation in stewardship by their own giving. Although churches do not designate what the pledge amount should be, it makes sense that session members should give as generously as possible since they formulate and establish the budget and program of the church and need to provide a model of Christian stewardship.

Deacons can easily find themselves making as many commitments as elders. Since the role of the Board of Deacons is defined as one "of sympathy, witness, and service after the example of Jesus Christ," its work is intensively people oriented. "Persons of spiritual character, honest repute, of exemplary lives, brotherly and sisterly love, warm sympathies, and sound judgment should be chosen for this office" (G-6.0401).

Usually the deacons exert most of their efforts in caring for the congregation, in cooperation with the pastor or pastors of the church. Often this board will be divided into geographic zones that permit a certain number of members to be assigned to each deacon for regular contact and pastoral care in times of illness or crisis. Deacons often have subcommittees that help members who are in the hospital, shut-in, or chronically ill. In many congregations, the deacons organize a system of ushers for various services of worship, to raise funds to assist those in financial distress, or to work with the pastors to establish and maintain food shelves or freezer meals for members and nonmembers in times of emergency. Deacons may also join the pastors in leading worship and assisting with the Lord's Supper.

Trustees. Because much of the work of the trustees involves the fiscal, administrative, and institutional aspects of the church, members who have extensive backgrounds in management, personnel, insurance, budget and accounting, fund raising, investments, property and grounds, and similar experience in business often make excellent members of the board. The committee structure of the Board of Trustees often includes Finance, Buildings and Grounds (if the session does not have this committee), Personnel (office and custodial), and Endowments (usually in concert with the session). Often the trustees are concerned with building security and the implementation of policies developed by the session for the use of the building(s) of the church by members and outside groups. Trustees usually serve on the Interpretation and Stewardship committee and on the session budget committee (along with committee chairpersons and other members of the church) as an annual challenge budget is developed to present to the congregation before pledges are solicited. The Board of Trustees obviously needs to be involved in the development and implementation of capital repairs and long-range plans for major plant renovations and construction.

Questions for Study

1. What are the most important duties of each of the elected officers, in your opinion?

2. *Do you think a person who has been ordained as an elder could also be qualified to be a trustee?*
3. *How many boards and committees should a member serve on at a time? How many night meetings do you think a church officer or a pastor should be required to attend during the course of a week? Is it possible that officers and pastors could spend too much time at the church, thereby destroying personal and family time? How much is too much? What can the church do to make the workload more healthy for all concerned?*

Who Works with Church Officers?
Other Staff and Elected and Volunteer Positions in the Church

Secretarial and Office Staff

Most congregations, regardless of size, have employees other than the pastor(s) who work closely with the officers. They have been hired because it is understood by the session and the congregation that there is important work that they have been called to accomplish for the church. Although these positions are not recognized by ordination, they must be treated with honor and respect and receive adequate compensation for their work.

Most churches (even with the advent of personal computers in church offices) enjoy the services of secretaries and/or other office personnel who provide administrative support for the pastors, staff, officers, and committees. On many occasions it is the voice on the telephone or the friendly face in the office that makes the initial impression of the church on a visitor. Secretaries and administrative personnel also usually provide the first contact a person has before seeing a pastor for counseling. Because of this front-line presence, this staff is able to read the heart of church members and keep others informed about vital congregational concerns. Office staff provided critical communication for the church, not only by publishing the newsletter, composing and updating the Internet home page, and answering the telephone, but by providing a daily, stable environment that keeps the church running cheerfully and efficiently. Office staff are key ambassadors in the church, and members must constantly be alert to the vital service they provide the ministry of Christ.

Christian Educators

In many churches, Christian education directors also provide important direction, leadership, and resources for the entire congregation. As the *Book of Order* puts it, "Christian educators are persons who demonstrate their faith in and love for Jesus Christ, are dedicated to the life of faith and are serious in purpose, honest in character, and joyful in service" (G-14.0701a). Whether they are full- or part-time, Christian educators often provide staff support to the committee which supervises the Christian education program in the church, usually including elementary church school, confirmation classes, and youth groups. "Christian educators will perform a variety of tasks including teaching the Bible, recommending curriculum materials and resources, training and supporting lay workers, and planning and administering the educational program of their congregations. Christian educators are accountable to the session and under the supervision of the pastor" (G-14.0701b).

Although the session has the responsibility to decide what experience and education are required of Christian educators serving a particular congregation, it is possible for people holding these positions to obtain the title of Certified Christian Educator through an accreditation process provided by the General Assembly (G-14.0703). Certified Christian Educators are granted the privilege of the floor (without vote) at presbytery meetings.

During the past few years, a number of General Assemblies have debated whether or not Christian educators should be ordained within the Presbyterian church. Thus far, the matter has been decided negatively, but it seems just and wise to consider that if we are willing to entrust the future of the church into the hands of our educators, the church should be willing to recognize their ministry as a true calling of God that should be honored by the laying on of hands.

Music Personnel

Most congregations have paid (sometimes volunteer) organists who lead the congregation in weekly worship through their music ministry. Standards of salary and payments for weddings, funerals, and other services not included in contracts are usually determined in accordance with recommendations by the American Guild of Organists.

Larger churches often have full-time or part-time directors of music who conduct the adult choir, supervise the organist and other music staff, and work closely with the pastors and Christian educators. Since music is often a vital part of youth Christian education programs, some congregations will also develop positions for bell choir directors, youth choir directors, and staff who direct special concerts and musical presentations.

The Directory for Worship reminds us how important the music ministry is in the Reformed concept of worship. "To lead the congregation in the singing of prayer is a primary role of the choir and other musicians. They also may pray on behalf of the congregation with introits, responses, and other musical forms. Instrumental music may be a form of prayer since words are not essential to prayer. In worship, music is not to be for entertainment or artistic display. Care should be taken that it not be used merely as a cover for silence. Music as prayer is to be a worthy offering to God on behalf of the people" (W-2.1004).

Youth Directors

One of the most challenging areas of church programming in American churches is often found in the area of youth ministry. Overburdened pastors and officers find that they do not have the time (or, if they are honest, the desire) to attract junior and senior high youth to activities in the church. Many congregations find that one solution is to hire a full- or part-time youth director to staff this important function. Churches that cannot afford the salary and benefits might consider the possibility of joining forces with nearby churches. In one city of 10,000 in upstate New York, the Episcopal, Lutheran, and Presbyterian churches have pooled funds, pastoral support, and volunteers to hire one youth director to provide common programs for all three churches. Such an approach saves money, uses the time of pastors and officers efficiently, and is a lot more fun for the youth involved.

Youth directors who are adequately trained and have the correct theological background are not easy to find in most communities. Churches will want to draw up careful job descriptions and precise person descriptions to make sure the directors relate well to youth, are mature enough to deal with anticipated problems and opportunities, and are able to work cooperatively with other adults.

Custodians

The position of custodian is a crucial one in most churches, but those who fill this vital role are often not given the recognition they deserve. Next to the secretary, the custodian may be the person that members see on the most regular basis. Custodians are true members of the ministry team. They do more than clean and secure the building. Often they are asked to move things at the last minute, carry boxes for the rummage sale, or fix a bruised knee on youth night. Custodians who are friendly, flexible, and loving members of the congregation are wonderful assets in the church family and should be appreciated as persons who truly minister in Christ's name.

Elected Personnel

The clerk of session is an elder who is elected by the session to record transactions at session and congregational meetings, keep rolls of membership and attendance, and preserve records carefully (G-9.0203). Although the clerk may be currently serving on the session, it is not necessary for him or her to do so. Many sessions decide that it is preferable to have a clerk who is not a session member, so that he or she can concentrate on necessary constitutional duties. In some churches, the clerk often serves as a primary advisor to the pastor(s) and may serve as a member of a session executive committee or comparable group.

The church treasurer is elected annually by the session (G-10.0401) and may be supervised by that body, or by the board of deacons or the trustees, as the session chooses. The treasurer generally is responsible for maintaining the financial procedures of the church and supervising volunteers and/or employees responsible for writing checks, counting and posting offerings, keeping financial books, and arranging for an annual audit. Often he or she also meets monthly with the session and trustees, is in frequent communication with the moderator of session, and may serve on the endowment and budget committees. Overall financial responsibility is shared in the Presbyterian Church. The session sets the budget and determines financial principles, though churches with trustees usually request them to monitor the budget and endowments. And since responsibilities are shared, it is necessary for the treasurer to maintain open communication between the two bodies to facilitate understanding and avoid conflict.

The moderator of the Board of Deacons is elected (usually annually) from among its members (G-6.0403). His or her duties (like those of the moderator of a session, presbytery, synod, or General Assembly) are to preserve order in the meetings of the deacons, conduct business efficiently, and call special meetings as necessary (G-9.0202). Since the pastors of the church are advisory members without vote (G-6.0403a), the moderator needs to work closely with the pastor who is assigned as staff to the deacons, to help facilitate and coordinate the caring ministry of the church. The moderator may also serve on the session executive committee in larger churches to foster communication and may be asked to serve on the budget committee.

The chairperson of the Board of Trustees. When a church has a separate board of trustees, a chairperson is usually elected annually from its own members. The chairperson needs to be in close communication with the moderator of the session, the treasurer, and the custodial and office staff in order to maintain the flow of information between the trustees and committees within the church. Often he or she is asked to serve on a session executive committee. If so, the moderator of the session keeps him or her informed of anticipated changes or problems within the church.

Questions for Study

1. *How is communication maintained among the various elected leaders of your church?*
2. *What provision is made to be sure on a monthly basis that each board is kept informed about the actions of all the boards?*

Contracted Volunteer Positions

Most congregations are able to save money and utilize the gifts and talents of members through the use of volunteers. In a sense, the bulk of the work of any church is accomplished by people who do not get paid. Church officers, youth group leaders, church school teachers, choir members, people who fold bulletins and put postage on the monthly newsletter are all working for free.

One way to make best use of volunteers is to create contracted volunteer positions. In churches where needed positions have insufficient money in the budget to support them, the pastor and session draw up specific job descriptions. Then selected volunteers sign a contract agreeing to work for a predetermined number of hours per week for a certain length of time (perhaps for a two-year period). Many churches find this to be a satisfactory way to solve staffing problems, and skilled people who are not currently employed (members between jobs, or retired men and women) are often pleased to use their skills in such a structured way.

Some positions that can be filled this way are Building and Maintenance Supervisor (someone to supervise the custodial staff on a daily basis and maintain building security); Office Administrator (works with the secretary and pastor in ordering supplies and in supervision of contract management); or Communications Director (edits the church newsletter, supervises the use of voice mail, constructs and maintains the church's home page on the Internet, and supervises church advertising). The development of creative and responsible volunteer positions assists the church immensely, gives volunteers satisfaction, and often helps members build their skills and résumés.

Questions for Study

1. *Does your church have ways in which it recognizes and thanks employees and volunteers annually?*

2. *What should the attitude of church members be toward church staff? Should they be regarded as employees or as partners in ministry?*

3. *Do you know how your church personnel committee evaluates employees and volunteers?*

Chapter 3

The Principles behind the *Book of Order* and the Form of Government

Introduction: *The Book of Order*

*T*he *Constitution* of the Presbyterian Church (U.S.A.) consists of two books (G-1.0500). The *Book of Confessions* (Part I) includes eleven historic confessions in the Reformed tradition (see chapter 4), and the *Book of Order* (Part II) is made up of the Form of Government, the Directory for Worship, and the Rules of Discipline.

When we try to explain what this order is we often resort to the slogan we see on T-shirts at General Assembly or presbytery meetings that say "Presbyterians Do It Decently and in Order" (in most places there are plenty of jokes about what "it" is).

The fact is, of course, that this motto is based on 1 Corinthians 14:40, where Paul summarizes his approach to speaking in tongues: "all things should be done decently and in order." The implication is that without order there is disorder; without decency there is strife, impoliteness, and lack of consideration.

The phrase Paul uses is *kata taxin*, which means "in order," "in an orderly manner." In *1 Clement* 40.1 (probably written just prior to 100 A.D.), the same concept is used to describe the way God appointed an "orderly fashion" of worship for the Jews by directing offerings to be made at certain times. The noun *taxis* is closely related to a verb meaning "to appoint, order, arrange" (*tassō*), and refers (in

Luke 7:1–10) to the Roman legions and their command structure (see v. 8).

When John Calvin was organizing his church in Geneva in the sixteenth century, he observed that there is nothing more important than order in establishing government, because of the great danger in doing things irregularly.[1] Churches, in his opinion, are best sustained when all things are under a well-ordered constitution. Thus Paul's injunction for decency and order is carried out when a church has definite regulations established through a "bond of union."[2]

Calvin gives important warnings, however. Constitutions are not to be considered necessary for salvation or to be substituted for the worship of God. They are a way of achieving God's will, but they are not to taken so seriously that they are held in absolute veneration. They must also have a certain amount of flexibility, since they need to accommodate the customs of each nation and age and allow for the establishment of new practices in place of old ones. His advice concerning the wisest method of change is still powerful: we will be safe if we let love be our guide.[3]

Calvin's theological principles of church government were incorporated by John Knox and the other founders of the Church of Scotland in the *First Book of Discipline* (1560) and later by others in its revision of 1592.[4] In this second version, church courts were established, including sessions, presbyteries, synods, and the General Assembly.

The organization created in Scotland was codified when the Westminster Assembly in England created the *Form of Presbyterial Church Government* in 1645.[5] It was also used as a basis of polity when the Presbytery of Philadelphia was founded in 1706. The *Form of Government and Discipline* was approved in the United States in 1788 when the General Synod adopted the constitution of the church and divided itself into four synods. The first General Assembly met in America on May 24, 1789, at Second Presbyterian Church in Philadelphia.[6]

Any institution, if it is to function effectively, needs organization and policies. The *Book of Order*, based on more than two hundred years of Presbyterian experience in church government and worship, guides congregations and higher governing bodies in routine decision making. It is the result of careful thought and prayer by elders and pastors who learned from Scripture and practice how to govern the church.

The *Book of Order* (along with the *Book of Confessions*) is the document that helps meld a diverse group of believers into the unity that makes us all Presbyterians. It defines a congregation, instructs officers about their duties, gives directions about the church and its property, describes the functions of the various governing bodies, sets standards for ordination and ecumenical relationships, provides a Directory for Worship, and sets forth guidelines for settling disputes (Rules of Discipline).

Because many Presbyterians value personal freedom very highly, they are often tempted to disregard the *Book of Order* when provisions do not suit them. This is a dangerous practice because it can create a dog that bites all masters. A member of session many want to avoid restrictions about infant baptism because he wishes his grandchild to be baptized (W-2.3014), even though the child's parents are not members. Later, however, he is shocked when another elder wants to limit the pastor's preaching (W-1.4005) and when she argues that one part of the *Book of Order* can be ignored as easily as the next. To avoid this kind of inconsistency, moderators and governing bodies always need to abide by the directives that the *Book of Order* sets out. The *Book of Order* insures uniformity of decision making across the whole nation, so that, whether one is a member of a congregation in Arkansas or Alaska or a commissioner to a synod in New Mexico or New York, similar decisions are all made in the same way. The church is not well served if individuals or governing bodies ignore or flout parts of the *Constitution* that seem outdated. If change is sought, the provisions for amendment must be implemented and discussed throughout the whole church, with the prayer that the Holy Spirit will help make necessary changes (see G-18.0000 and the discussion at the end of this chapter).

Recently this concept of church order has been tested almost to the breaking point by the debate (since 1978) concerning the ordination of gay and lesbian members. It remains to be seen whether a church can hold together when the issue dividing it goes far beyond questions of polity and ignites disruptive disagreements about fundamental values and touches the deepest nerves of faith, interpretation of the Word, and the concept of justice before God.[7] Some Presbyterians say truth is the primary concern in this issue. Others say it is order and the proper understanding of Scripture. A third group argues that what really matters is justice, fairness, and the love and mercy of Christ. If members are acknowledged to be equal in the church, why are some members more equal than others? Although wise voices counsel the church to take its time and let the Spirit work, advising those who want change to wait for the proper day to come, others wonder how long the church can remain silent while some members are deprived of access to church office? How long is too long when the church stands divided over an issue so crucial to the lives of so many members?

Questions for Study

1. *What is the balance between order and freedom in the Presbyterian Church? What issues test it in your church?*

2. *Which is more important for you in the church, discipline or enthusiasm?*

3. *Can you think of examples in the life of the church today where discipline is vitally important?*

4. *In the case of ordination of officers and the proper interpretation of scriptures how should we apply "the rule of faith and love" in the Second Helvetic Confession (C-5.010)?*

The Historic Heart of Presbyterian Government

Many attempts have been made to summarize the heart of Presbyterian church government. At various times it was capsulized in two simple words, *order* and *ardor*. These concepts were thought to be more than enough to describe our adherence to a church of uniform government and our enthusiasm and love for the spreading of the gospel and propagation of the justice of Christ. According to David McCarthy, however, the theological principles behind Presbyterian polity can be better understood when expanded to four essentials:

> Order
> The equality of all people before God
> Accountability
> Discipline[8]

In the *Manual of Presbyterian Law for Church Officers and Members* (1950), the general principles of the church are defined at even greater length:

> That Christ is the only Head of the Church;
> that all true believers are in union with Christ as their Head;
> that Christ has appointed a government in his Church;
> that the right inheres in all believers, as members of Christ's body, to participate in church affairs;
> that the Church possesses authority to discipline offenders and to administer government;
> that Christians have the right to associate voluntarily together in denominations and to prescribe terms of communion;
> that all denominations holding the essentials of the Christian religion are to be recognized as Churches of Christ;
> and that the ideal ecclesiastical organization is "a free Church in a free State."[9]

Chapters I–IV as Bedrock

No matter how Presbyterian government is defined, an appreciation of the first four chapters of the Form of Government is essential for a correct understanding of our life together.

The first chapter begins with the best starting point: all power in the church begins with Jesus Christ. The church universal and the Presbyterian Church (U.S.A.) have no other Head, CEO, President, Moderator, or Director, and need none. Jesus is the Lord of all Christians and of all Presbyterians, and it is his body that is called and empowered to do his work (G-1.0100).

In the second section of chapter 1, "The Great Ends of the Church," the six major purposes for the church's existence are carefully enumerated:

- the salvation of humankind
- the shelter, nurture, and spiritual fellowship of the children of God
- the maintenance of divine worship
- the preservation of truth
- the promotion of social righteousness
- and the exhibition of the Kingdom of Heaven to the world

In 1997 the 209th General Assembly called all Presbyterians to use "The Great Ends" as the basis of the church's reflections and actions during 1998–2003, and provided study resources, bulletins, and banner designs to help congregations and governing bodies focus on these essential goals of the church's life.[10] As a joint report to the 1997 Assembly put it,

> These words were first adopted by the United Presbyterian Church of North America at the turn of the century. They are our church's common understanding of Christ's call to us for faithful discipleship. They express the common ground of Presbyterian mission. They are right on target with the needs of our world as we enter yet another new century. Evangelical fervor is linked with a passion for social justice. The nurture of community is linked with fidelity to God's truth. Our worship is linked to how we exhibit God's love for the world in our daily life. Now is the time for all Presbyterians to reclaim this vision as our common ground.[11]

The third section of the Form of Government's introduction to Presbyterian polity, "The Historic Principles of Church Order"

(G-1.0300), was originally adopted by the Synod of New York and Philadelphia in 1788 and describes what Eugene Carson Blake called the "two-part heritage of all the members of the Presbyterian Church": freedom and responsibility under the law.[12] These eight principles of church order include aspects of church government that can be traced back to Scottish concepts of freedom and representative law that influenced the framers of the U.S. Constitution. They include the following:

1. Freedom of conscience is a fundamental right ("God alone is Lord of conscience"; G-1.0301), together with the separation of church and state.
2. Every church has the right to establish the terms of admission into its fellowship, and the qualifications of its ministers and members.
3. Jesus Christ appointed officers, not only to preach and administer the sacraments, but to exercise discipline.
4. Truth is in order to goodness.
5. People of good conscience can have different opinions, and all Christians and all societies need to exercise mutual forbearance toward each other (G-1.0305).
6. The right to elect members of a society rests in that society (G-1.0307).
7. The Holy Scriptures are the only rule of faith and conduct.
8. An ecclesiastical body receives its authority from its own spiritual and moral power, which rests solely on its own justice (rather than the force of civil government), the approval of the public, and the blessing of Jesus Christ (G-1.0308).

The fourth section of chapter 1 of the Form of Government was adopted in 1797 by the General Assembly.[13] "The Historic Principles of Church Government" contains the four "radical" (or fundamental) guidelines for ecclesiastical discipline that are derived from Scripture and the practice of the early church:

• that several different congregations constitute one church of Christ

- that a larger part of the church, or a representation of it, should govern the smaller
- that a majority should govern
- that complaints and appeals should be made from lower to higher courts and that final decisions should be made by the "collected wisdom and united voice of the whole Church"

These historic foundation stones are joined in chapter 4 into the nine Principles of Presbyterian Government, which include the following:

- Individual churches make up the one church known as the Presbyterian Church (U.S.A.).
- The church is governed by presbyters (elders).
- Presbyters not only represent the will of the people who elect them, but also the will of God.
- Decisions shall be reached, after discussion, by vote, and the majority shall rule.
- Higher governing bodies will have rights of review and control over lower ones.

The Second Part of the Form of Government

The second part of the Form of Government consists of four sections in which the historic principles are worked out in practical detail. In the first two sections, the church outlines the rights, privileges, and limitations of the local congregation, the session, and the higher governing bodies, as well as their interactions with one another. These are the Local Church (chapters V–VIII) and Governing Bodies (IX–XIII).

The last two sections contain detailed outlines on the theology and practice of ordaining and recognizing church workers (chapter XIV) and the principles of participating in ecumenical and interfaith ministry (chapters XV–XVII). The chapters on relationships with other denominations, union churches, and union presbyteries provide an appropriate conclusion to a part of the *Constitution* that begins with the Lordship of Jesus Christ in the universal church. Presbyterians understand that even though they have a form of government with biblical and historical antecedents, they do not possess the only way in which Christ's church can be organized. Indeed, as we seek "to initiate, maintain, and strengthen . . . relations to, and engage in mission with, other Presbyterian and Reformed bodies and with other Christian churches, alliances, councils, and consortia" (G-15.0102), we anticipate a new century when we may more fully realize practical ways in which we are called "to a new openness to God's continuing reformation of the Church ecumenical, that it might be a more effective instrument of mission in the world" (G-3.0401d). The 1999 "Formula of Agreement" between the Presbyterian Church (U.S.A.), the Evangelical Lutheran Church in America, the Reformed Church in America, and the United Church of Christ (as well as the conversations between Episcopalians and Lutherans) are harbingers of this new world.

Questions for Study

1. What are the similarities between the Great Ends, the Principles of Church Order, and the Principles of Presbyterian Government? What are the differences?

2. Can you think of any of the Great Ends of the Church that need to receive more emphasis today?

3. If we believe that Christ is present in the church and is truly its Head, how do these convictions influence the day-to-day operation of the church or the presbytery? If they do not, how should they?

Changing the *Book of Order*

The *Book of Order* is a compendium of Presbyterian experience based on more than two hundred years of practice, prayer, and study of Scripture. Occasionally, church officers form the mistaken opinion that it is a static document, forever fixed by someone in the presbytery or General Assembly. In fact, the *Book of Order* is designed to be very fluid, constantly open to amendment, change, and reform. As the *Book of Order* itself says, "The Presbyterian Church (U.S.A.) would be faithful to the Lordship of Christ and to its historic tradition of the Church reformed always reforming, by the Spirit of God. In this faith, amendment procedures are understood as a means to faithfulness as God breaks forth yet more light from God's Word" (G-18.0101).

What if an individual, a session, a presbytery, or a commissioner to General Assembly does not like part of the *Book of Order*? There are several options which make it possible for us to change the way we govern ourselves.

First, it is always wise to make sure we have understood the exact intent of the provision in question. A good way to start is by referring to the *Book of Order, Annotated Edition*,[14] which is available through the Presbyterian Distribution Service. It provides information about all the changes and interpretations incorporated in the *Book of Order* since 1983 and gives necessary historical perspective.

Further questions about changes may be answered most easily by a pastor, the executive presbyter, the stated clerk of the presbytery, or the synod's stated clerk. Particularly difficult inquiries may be directed to the Office of the General Assembly, Department of Constitutional Services, in Louisville or to the Office of the Stated Clerk.

It is possible for the amendment process to begin at the grassroots level. If individual members or elders on the session think that a provision of the *Book of Order* needs to be changed, they may write an "overture" suggesting the altered wording. If the session passes the overture it may be sent to the presbytery. The presbytery may reject, accept, or change it. Individual commissioners and committees of presbytery may also submit overtures for presbytery consideration, following whatever process a presbytery has established. If it is accepted in some form, it is sent to the Stated Clerk of the General Assembly at least 120 days prior to the next session of General Assembly (G-18.0300). The Clerk will then refer the amendment to the Advisory Committee on the Constitution (G-13.0112) and this committee will report it to the General Assembly with recommendations or proposed emendations. If the overture is approved by the General Assembly, it is sent to each presbytery for vote during the next year (along with other proposed overtures). If a majority of the presbyteries approve the changes, the succeeding General Assembly shall declare the amendment made and the *Book of Order* is changed in its next printing. Overtures may also be initiated by a synod or special committees of the General Assembly.[15]

Similarly, the *Book of Confessions* may also be amended. Proposed amendments are reviewed by the General Assembly. If approved, they are recommended to the presbyteries, where they must be approved in writing by a two-thirds vote. The new amendments do not take force until they are approved and enacted by the General Assembly meeting in the next year. G-18.0201b requires that before such amendments may be sent to the presbyteries, the General Assembly must appoint a committee of elders and ministers to review the proposal. This committee will consult with the committee or governing body in which the amendment originated, then report its recommendations to the next General Assembly.

Each year, presbytery commissioners receive a booklet of proposed overtures to the *Constitution* that reflect a spirit of change, improvement, and reform in a living church. It is exciting to see how the Spirit works afresh to help the church of Christ adjust to changing times and needs, making it a church reformed, always being reformed by God (G-2.0200).

Chapter 4

In the Spirit:
The Directory for Worship

Introduction: Presbyterian Worship Resources

*I*n most Presbyterian churches there are unopened treasures waiting to be discovered. They are not hidden under a bushel or locked in a vault but are in plain view for all to see, though they are unknown and unappreciated by most church members. We call these treasures the Directory for Worship and the *Book of Common Worship*.

The Directory for Worship was added to the *Constitution* in 1989 to replace the Directory for the Service of God, which had been included in the *Book of Order* created by the reuniting churches in 1983. Its history can be traced through several rewrites and revisions, all the way back to the first directory published in the United States in 1788, then back to the Westminster *Directory of Worship* (1644) and to John Knox's service (following John Calvin) in the *Book of Common Order* (1556).

The most recent Directory for Worship was published following careful study, after the editors were directed by the 1983 General Assembly to keep in mind ten guidelines. It was to

1. Reflect biblical understandings of the human response to God's presence and action in the life of the world;
2. Be guided by the faith and practice of the church through the ages;

3. Be guided by that heritage that frees us to resist imposed forms, but constrains us to obey God's Word in matters of worship;
4. Be informed by our Reformed confessions;
5. Be in scope and orientation catholic rather than sectarian;
6. Be open to the richness of traditional and cultural ways of responding to God's grace;
7. Assure an openness to the Holy Spirit's creativity, which is spontaneous yet orderly;
8. Emphasize worship as the work of all the people, whose different gifts are expressed through different functions and offices;
9. Recognize that as we faithfully worship God, the Holy Spirit calls and sends us to bear witness to Jesus Christ in the world through grateful and obedient service;
10. Be the product of reflection, debate and consideration by the whole church.

The Directory for Worship "describes the theology that underlines Reformed worship and outlines appropriate forms for that worship." It "suggests possibilities for worship, invites development in worship, and encourages continuing reform of worship" (Preface).

The *Book of Common Worship*, on the other hand, provides actual suggested orders of worship, special services, and prayers to be used in the weekly or seasonal worship of the church. Published in 1993 by the Presbyterian Church (U.S.A.) and the Cumberland Presbyterian Church,[1] this book also has a rich history stretching back to the work of John Knox. The first *Book of Common Worship* in the United States was approved by the Presbyterian Church in the U.S.A. (northern) in 1906, with revisions in 1932 and 1946. In 1970 *The Worshipbook—Services*, a thorough revision, was prepared by the Joint Committee on Worship, which this time included the Presbyterian Church in the United States.[2]

Presbyterians often wonder what is meant when we call our

prayer book "common." This title, frequently associated with Reformed worship, refers to the fact that in addition to the inclusion of contemporary materials, elements are also drawn from the history of Christian worship, demonstrating that "prayers and forms shared in common with the church from other times and places give a sense of our unity with the people of God throughout time" (Preface, *Book of Common Worship*).

Both the Directory for Worship and the *Book of Common Worship* provide invaluable spiritual and theological resources for public and private worship. They reflect the depth and variety of worship possibilities within our denomination and within the Reformed tradition, and prepare our hearts to encounter God in new and old ways. What is said in the excellent preface of the *Book of Common Worship* applies to both resources. They are "offered to the church with a fervent prayer that [they] may be . . . effective aid[s] to congregations as they worship God, and . . . further the renewal of the church's faith and life."[3]

Questions for Study

1. *Does your church use the* Book of Common Worship *in weekly worship? How is it used?*

2. *Has your session or worship/music committee used the Directory for Worship for study at its meetings? How could it be utilized to help enrich worship?*

Word and World

One of the most powerful, compelling, and inspiring aspects of the Directory for Worship is its intentional linking of worship with commitment to the mission of Jesus Christ in the world. As the first sentence of the preface states, "This Directory for Worship reflects the conviction that the life of the Church is one, and that its worship, witness, and service are inseparable." Indeed, most Presbyterian churches follow an order of worship that has three basic segments in which worshipers gather first around the

Word, proclaim and hear it, then bear and follow it into the world (W-3.3202).

The implication seems clear: there can be no worship without mission and outreach; there can be no worship that is centered on the self or the individual church. To be in communication with Jesus Christ is to go into the world he loves. This important connection is particularly emphasized in the last chapter but is found in principle throughout the Directory. As chapter VII points out, the church is called by God to participate in mission through its proclamation and evangelism, through the expression of compassion, by working for justice and peace, by caring for creation and life as it preserves and protects the environment (ecojustice), and by acknowledging the present reality of God's reign and its promised fulfillment in the future.

Elsewhere, we are continually reminded that worship goes far beyond strengthening the individual or merely creating fellowship in the body. Presbyterian worship provides nurture and education that equips members to live as commissioned disciples in the world and leads to "world awareness," calling all to be responsible citizens and servants of God (W-6.2001n–.2003). It urges worshipers to give themselves to God by offering their lives, their particular gifts and abilities, and their material goods (W-2.5001). Members not only express concern for events in their own daily lives, but also for ministry in the world (W-2.6001). Prayers are regularly offered for the church universal, for those in distress, for the nation, the state, and local communities (W-3.3506). Concern for the world is also expressed in mission interpretation as part of worship (W-3.5601), in fasting, keeping vigil, and other forms of "enacted prayer" (W-5.5003), especially in preparation for acts of discipleship such as penitence, reconciliation, peacemaking, social protest, and compassion (see W-5.4002).

The Directory for Worship does not envision different kinds of worshiping communities: those that keep to themselves and those that work in the world. "The church in worship proclaims, receives, and enacts reconciliation in Jesus Christ and commits itself to strive for justice and peace in its own life and in the world" (W-7.4001). In worship, children begin to learn what justice means; in prayer, the faithful lift up those who experience brokenness, violence, and injustice; and in worship, they commit and prepare themselves "to be reconcilers seeking justice and pursuing peace" (W-7.4004).

Questions for Study

1. *How would you answer those who argue that before we help people in other countries we should take care of our own first?*

2. *Do you think a church can legitimately exist without local mission? Can it call itself a church of Jesus Christ if it does not extend itself into all the world?*

Language about God and People

One of the weaknesses of *The Worshipbook* (1970)[4] was that the language used in its prayers and hymns was outdated almost before it was published. The Directory for Worship (1989), *The Presbyterian Hymnal* (1990),[5] and the *Book of Common Worship* (1993) all clearly aim to correct that defect.

Those who were pastors and elders in the 1970s and 1980s can remember vividly the ferment in the churches and on the floors of presbyteries about using inclusive language for God and for other worshipers. Old habits do not die quickly, and the church was accustomed to using masculine terms for God and male pronouns for all the people of God, whether they were men or women. Pastors struggled in sermons and prayers to stop referring to parishioners and the rest of humanity as "men," and fierce debates erupted at presbytery meetings and at various General Assembly meetings about the correct way to address God. Clergy and pastors had to be sensitized repeatedly to the new demands of inclusive language. Presbyteries and synods sponsored debates and seminars to demonstrate something that

Presbyterians claimed to believe already: women are equal partners in ministry and deserve equal respect.

As the preface of the *Book of Common Worship* puts it, "Care was taken in the development . . . that its language be inclusive, not only in reference to the people of God but also in language about God and address to God. Guidelines for inclusive language adopted by the General Assembly in 1975, 1979, 1980, and 1985 were implicitly followed in the preparation of the texts." Similarly *The Presbyterian Hymnal* adopts a guideline to ensure that hymn texts are inclusive of all God's people and sensitive to age, race, gender, physical limitations, and language.[6]

Regarding the Directory for Worship, editors were charged with the responsibility of finding new modes of expression while retaining traditional biblical images. Daniel B. Wessler said, "Language was a *now* dimension for the Directory Task Force to come to grips with. For twenty years the church had been producing guiding papers on faith forming language about God and the people of God. Now it was time for authoritative guidelines about the use of inclusive language in worship and about the amplification of language about God that would reflect many rich and varied metaphors for God imbedded in the biblical account of the relation between God and God's people."[7]

In the Directory for Worship, Presbyterians are urged to continue to use trinitarian language (W-1.1001–.1002) and God is spoken of as creator, begetter, and bearer (1.2003), the risen Lord Jesus Christ (1.2004), and the Spirit who leads the church to develop new forms of worship (1.2005). In particular, biblical images of God are examined to show that desired changes in the language about God are already found in Scripture (see "Old Testament Symbols," 1.2003). A similar list is made of New Testament symbols and Jesus' use of words about God (1.2004), although more could have been said about New Testament images referring to God in feminine terms (see Matt. 23:37; Luke 13:34; and 1 Thess. 2:7, for example). At the end of the section on language we are reminded that "The church shall strive in its worship to use language about God which is intentionally as diverse and varied as the Bible and our theological traditions. The church is committed to using language in such a way that all members of the community of faith may recognize themselves to be included, addressed, and equally cherished before God" (1.2006b).

The use of inclusive language for God in hymns, prayers, and everyday speech continues to be extremely important. It not only allows us to praise God according to God's true nature but it leads to respect for each other and our diversity and individual gifts. Chances are, if we have a narrow definition of God, we will think we are justified in building a fence around the church that is designed to keep out people who do not meet our prescriptions for acceptability. The way in which we name God often determines the measure of respect we are able to give to people who are different from us.

Questions for Study

1. *How do you like to sing hymns that refer to God as "Father" or "He"? Does it make any difference if you are a woman or a man?*

2. *Being male and female is of great significance in American culture. How important is it in the kingdom of God?*

The Broad Range of Inclusiveness

The use of inclusiveness in worship applies to more than our descriptions of God or the simple use of language about one another. We are also called to treat each other with respect, include all believers within the circle of faith, and display the rich varieties, cultures, forms, actions, and settings of worship we share as Presbyterians within our worship (W-1.2006).

Appropriate language about people involves more than technical correctness about ethnic origin or gender. It reflects our knowledge that we are all loved by God and saved by Jesus Christ. It demonstrates our respect for the unity of the worldwide church and God's concern for all children of faith.

It may go further than that. When leaders of other nations, especially those that have other majority religious groups, address the American people with greetings to all Christians and make positive references to Puritan religious principles used to found our nation (as President Mohammad Khatami of Iran did in 1998), we are usually drawn to listen. Regardless of political differences that may exist between the United States and other countries, we sense that these leaders are doing their best to make a connection between their religious communities and a Christian tradition of which we are a part. Their respect for our beliefs and history draws us into the communication process.

How we include other people in worship is reflected similarly not merely in the language we use, but in the way we speak to them and encourage them to express their faith according to their own experiences. This kind of inclusiveness involves communication among diverse cultures represented in the church (G-4.0401), as well as openness to the varieties of talents and gifts of all of God's people (G-4.0402). It involves how sermons are delivered (W-2.2007), whether children are included (W-3.1004), how prayers and scriptures are read (W-2.2005), and how music is performed (W-2.1003). One example of such inclusiveness is the availability of Native American and Korean stanzas in a few of our favorite hymns in *The Presbyterian Hymnal* (for example, "Amazing Grace" and "Blessed Assurance").

Broad inclusiveness also welcomes the participation of different kinds of people who believe in Jesus Christ into the membership, ministry, and worship of the church (W-1.2006). The *Book of Order* condemns an inability or unwillingness to do so in the strongest language: "Each member must seek the grace of openness in extending the fellowship of Christ to all persons. . . . Failure to do so constitutes a rejection of Christ himself and causes a scandal to the gospel" (G-5.0103).

C. Benton Kline summarizes the importance of maintaining a broad inclusiveness in the church's worship when he writes, "When forms, actions, languages, or settings of worship exclude the expression of diverse cultures actually represented in the church, they are unauthentic and inappropriate, false to the reality of Jesus Christ and false to the life of the church. And when . . . [they] deny the needs and identities of believers . . . then again they are unauthentic and inappropriate."[8]

Questions for Study

1. *How could music, prayers, and sermons be varied in our services of worship to be more culturally inclusive?*
2. *The Directory for Worship (W-3.1004) calls for the regular inclusion of children in worship and requires that the session ensure that the church does not prevent their participation. Do you think congregations that have children who leave halfway through a service to attend church school are abiding by this part of the* Constitution?
3. *Are there ethnic groups in your area who might be more inclined to worship with you if your service reflected their traditions more often?*

Worship, Space, and Place

When presbyteries meet, the hosting congregation is often asked to provide a brief history of its church for the packet that is mailed out to commissioners in advance. Usually the review gives a detailed account of the history of the church buildings (especially the construction of the sanctuary), various additions that were made, and the capital drives that were instituted to finance the changes. Occasionally the ministries of a few favorite pastors are also mentioned. Yet it is odd that the focus is on the history of buildings and worship space. If commissioners were inclined to read more critically, they might like to know who worshiped there, how they encountered God in that particular place, what service made their ministry in that location unique, and what issues of peace and justice they stood up for during their history in the service of Jesus Christ.

Buildings and sanctuaries are important to us. Most of our bulletin covers show that we identify church with a particular structure. Buildings provide predictability, focus, comfort, ease, and security. They make us feel at home. When pastors and members move to a new church they often feel a sense of loss because they are in new surroundings. Their children, if they are older, may feel particularly dislocated when they come back to be married. "How can we be married here?" they may ask. "The sanctuary isn't like the one in which we grew up. It just doesn't feel right (and anyway, it doesn't have a center aisle!)."

Considering the amount of money and time we invest in our buildings, we can see that the space where we worship, have fellowship, attend meetings, and educate our children is very important to us. It gives us a sense of concrete identity, making us feel that it is where most of our ministry takes place. The Directory for Worship has wise suggestions for the arrangement of worship space to assure a proper setting for accessibility, ease of gathering, and the integration of Word and Sacrament (W-1.3024).

Yet we have all had experiences that belie this attachment to buildings. If a building burns down or if a congregation has to relocate to a new part of a town or city, we discover that the building is not as important as we once thought. What is more, we know that the church building can be precisely the place where Christian ministry does not take place. Sometimes it is where we are the most unfaithful to God, where we decide not to follow Christ's leading, where we treat each other in the most un-Christlike manner. Being in a particular structure, familiar or not, does not guarantee that people will be treated with Christian love or respect. We deny our own faith when the church allows gossip to dominate the coffee hour, when employees are treated unfairly or without due process, or when members silently discriminate against others in the community who sense that they are not welcome, even though no one ever says so.

What is more, many people have experiences during worship in other settings that are more significant than what they have had in their familiar surroundings. In my own case, I have felt closest to God in the most unlikely locales: in a church in northern

Nicaragua where machine guns were propped up next to pews in anticipation of a possible *contra* raid; in a thatched roof hut in western Ethiopia where the dirt floors were covered with cow dung, the pews were simple planks, and the people sang their hearts out to God in pure joy accompanied by percussion instruments made of gourds filled with dried beans; in a quiet spot along the Jordan River which reminded me of Jesus' baptism; or in the Garden of Gethsemane, in the place where Jesus may have made the painful decision to surrender his life to God.

The Directory for Worship (W-1.3020–.3024) reminds us how important worship space is and how it should be arranged. But it also draws us back to the most fundamental concept that, even though we set aside special places for worship, in the last analysis "it is not the particular place, but the presence of the risen Lord in the midst of the community which marks the reality of worship" (W-1.3023). This reality may provoke Americans to pray in different ways if they are primarily attached to their property, building size, steeple height, and impressive addresses.

Questions for Study

1. *What is there about your sanctuary that makes you feel comfortable when you worship there? How do you feel if you visit another congregation?*

2. *Do you think you can worship as effectively out of doors, at a campsite, or on a mountain top?*

3. *Are some architectural styles more conducive to worship than others?*

The Importance of Daily Prayer

Some mornings pastors wake up and realize that one of the hardest things to learn is the discipline of daily prayer. Even though they may lead worship twice each Sunday and take part in prayer time during a weekly church staff meeting, and even though prayer may be a regular part of dinnertime each day, they may recognize that they need something more profound and sustaining.

The benefits of daily prayer are obvious: with stronger spiritual lives, we are closer to God, more confident in our work, of more use to friends and family, and more mature Christ-centered people all around. Yet we constantly fall in and out of the habit. Sometimes we think we are too busy, we do not feel like it, we get mad at God, we wonder if it will do any good.

The Directory for Worship reminds us that daily personal worship is a discipline for attending to God and accepting God's grace (W-5.2001). "An aspect of the discipline of daily personal worship is finding the times and places where one can focus on God's presence, hear God's Word, and respond to God's grace in prayer, self-offering, and commitment to service." Elsewhere we find suggestions about how we may express our personal prayers (W-5.4000). Or we are encouraged to involve our families in regular times of prayer (W-5.7000); or taught that Christians may worship at any time or any place (W-1.3011); or urged to be sure that our prayers are carried out and acted out in our lives (W-1.1005, 2.1005, 3.5403, 6.3011). The Directory for Worship even encourages local churches to offer Services of Daily Prayer throughout the week, although it is doubtful that many congregations do so (W-3.4000).

As church officers we are especially responsible to the church in our prayer life. All our congregations have problems in ministry that we should bring to God in prayer; members are ill and have deep concerns and need our daily support. And we all must pray for our pastors and other church leaders, and church school teachers; our leaders in presbyteries, synods, and General Assembly; our public school teachers and professors and administrators at our colleges and seminaries; and our community, state, and federal officials. We need to pray for our missionaries by name here and abroad, so they can do God's will each day. We could pray for writers and editors of church journals and for those who write books for the church to use. And we want to include our own family members in intercessory prayer and imagine them coming out of their difficulties with God's help. We must continually pray for the poor and oppressed—and pray without ceasing for peace.

As Oswald Chambers indicates in his writings, we often mistakenly assume that prayer only assists us in our work. But he abruptly reminds us: prayer is our work. "Prayer does not equip us for greater works—prayer is the greater work. Yet we think of prayer as some common sense exercise of our higher powers that simply prepares us for God's work. . . . Prayer *is* the battle, and it makes no difference where you are. However God may engineer your circumstances, your duty is to pray."[9]

Perhaps the following prayer will help church officers and pastors whenever they wonder why their energy level and enthusiasm is at a low ebb.

> *Dear God, sometimes life goes by so quickly,*
> *we hardly know where we are.*
> *So many decisions to make, so little time.*
> *Yet today we have these precious moments*
> *to reestablish contact with you.*
> *Help us to relax, reflect, and listen,*
> *enfolded in your love.*
> *Loving God,*
> *slow us down,*
> *heal us,*
> *give us ears to hear*
> *and hearts to feel*
> *your presence and your love.*
>   *In the name of Jesus Christ we pray, Amen.*

Questions for Study

1. *Why is it often difficult to maintain a disciplined prayer life?*

2. *Look at some of the passages in Scripture that describe Jesus' prayer life (Mark 1:35; Luke 9:18; 18:11; 22:41; Matt. 6:5–15; 17:21; 21:13; 21:22). How important was it to him?*

3. *Can you think of a time when prayer was of absolute significance to you? Are there times when it has been very
important to the life of your church, to our denomination?*

The Personal Spiritual Life

If a new Christian asked you how to begin a prayer life and
start a regular course of scripture reading, what would you
advise him or her to do? Such a question is asked so seldom in
a Presbyterian church these days that many of us might be
stunned. Yet even in our denomination, members do occasionally join the church because God has called them to Christ for
the first time—it happens once in a while in the most unlikely
congregations! And the answers we formulate to their questions
not only help them but give us insight into how we conduct our
own spiritual lives.

Fortunately the Directory for Worship provides good material
for answering this question for others and for ourselves. The
beginning of chapter 2 reminds us that prayer is the heart of worship; that in prayer we seek after and are found by the one true
God. It teaches us again (or for the first time) that prayer may be
spoken, sung, offered in silence, or enacted; that there are several types of prayer: adoration, thanksgiving, confession, supplication, intercession, and self-dedication. It is always a good test
of our own spiritual maturity, and an excellent way to help new
Christians learn the discipline of prayer, to define all six types
and discover how they may be used (or abused), if we discover
that we spend most of our time praying only for ourselves, or
those we love, or our own church.

Leslie Weatherhead developed a useful prayer method that
gives wonderful spatial images for those who like to go beyond
mere definitions to the *practice* of prayer.[10] Noting that Jesus
urged his followers to go into a private room and pray (Matt.
6:6), and remembering that most of the people who heard Jesus
only lived in one-room houses, Weatherhead pointed out that
Jesus was talking about going into a *symbolic room*. Using this

image as a building block, he developed an entire *house of prayer* to help people construct a useful daily prayer routine. The rooms he built include Room 1 ("Affirming the Presence of God"), Room 2 (A room on the east side of the house full of morning sunshine, where we praise, thank, and adore God), Room 3 (possibly the attic, where we examine the trunk full of memories, and then confess our sin and accept God's forgiveness), Room 4 (the room in which we relax most easily and are ourselves, set aside for affirmation and reception), Room 5 ("Purified Desire and Sincere Petition"), Room 6 (the family room, lined with photographs of people we are concerned about, the room where we pray for others), and Room 7 (the room at the top of the house set aside for meditation). Weatherhead also provides appropriate furniture (prayers, readings, and scriptures) for each room in this special house of prayer.

As for the second part of the new Christian's question—learning how to read the Bible—it is not advisable to tell people to begin at the beginning. The Bible is not a book; it is a library of books written over hundreds of years. And although it has far more to offer than an encyclopedia, few people would want to read a set going from A to Z. For people who have confessed their faith for the first time, it would be better to start with *Mark* (to know Christ better and absorb the details of his teaching and life), move on to *Acts* (to learn about the church), read *Galatians* (to get a small taste of Paul), look at *1 John* (to focus on the Christian concept of love), then try *Genesis*. New Christians should also be directed often to *Psalms*, to find help when they must face their own personal spiritual struggles. To assist them in their reading, it would be helpful to provide a copy of a general introduction to the Bible written for first readers. Since the Bible contains ancient books, we need a road map to find our way through its cultural, historical, and spiritual twists and turns. (Presumably we would do no less if we were trying to explore the riches of Shakespeare for the first time.) Perhaps it would also be useful to look at the Directory for Worship for what it tells us about the nature of the Bible and how to meditate on it and obey it more faithfully (W-5.3000). Perhaps it would be helpful for seasoned believers to join the students and read over the same books of the Bible in a fresh translation. Who knows? Perhaps we might see their contents through new eyes again, wrestle with the challenges and demands of the gospel, and be renewed and refreshed in our response to God and our commitment to do Christ's work (W-5.3002).

The Sacraments

In new-member classes or officer training groups there is often an uncomfortable silence if the leader asks, "How many sacraments do Presbyterians celebrate?" Since the Roman Catholic Church is strong all over our country, many Presbyterians actually think we have seven sacraments rather than two. Although we respect the value of confirmation, confession, marriage, ordination, and the anointing of the sick, we only celebrate the sacraments of baptism and the Lord's Supper, because they are the only ones initiated by Jesus.

A sacrament is not easy to define. The Directory for Worship uses a traditional definition taken from Reformed theology. "Sacraments are signs of the real presence and power of Christ in the Church, symbols of God's action. Through the Sacraments, God seals believers in redemption, renews their identity as the people of God, and marks them for service" (W-1.3033(2)). Similarly, Question 92 in the Westminster Shorter Catechism says that "A sacrament is a holy ordinance instituted by Christ, wherein, by sensible signs, Christ and the benefits of the new covenant are represented, sealed, and applied to believers."

John Calvin's definition seems less complicated and clearer. In a little book written in 1537 to help inspire a simple faith in the people of Geneva, Switzerland, he defines a sacrament as "an external sign through which the Lord presents and testifies to us his good will to us in order to sustain us in the weakness of our faith."[11] A shorter definition that Calvin elsewhere quotes from Augustine is even better: a sacrament is "a visible form of an invisible grace."[12]

"A visible form of an invisible grace"—by taking things

people used every day, material things they could see, smell, touch, eat, and drink, Jesus provided symbols of something that was invisible but just as real: the love and forgiveness of God in Jesus Christ.

Baptism

Baptism represents the cleansing action of God through the use of everyday water. By being baptized himself, Jesus taught, through his own actions, that people had to be cleansed by God. According to Matthew 28:16–20, just prior to returning to God after the resurrection, Jesus commanded his disciples to go into all the world and baptize in his name.

The word baptize comes from the Greek *baptizō*, which means simply "to dip under." In Jesus' day people dipped their dishes under water; so also they washed their hair, their babies, and their clothes. By employing a common verb and the water that people used for drinking and washing, Jesus recalled the covenant that God made with the people of Israel in the Old Testament.

Baptism is an exciting moment in any church. If an adult is baptized, we can be sure that he or she has thought carefully about confessing Jesus Christ as Lord and Savior for the first time. When they say, after they have joined the church, "I am happy to be a member of the congregation," we know they really mean it.

The baptism of children is very special too. Proud parents, happy grandparents, the innocence of the babies, the joy of a growing congregation, the knowledge that we are all loved by God—these things make baptism Sunday a festive occasion.

The Directory for Worship specifies, however, that not all children are eligible for baptism. Sometimes this causes confusion and pain in the church. For it is not the children who are ineligible, of course, but the parents' lack of membership in a Christian community that creates a very uncomfortable situation. As we read in W-2.3014, "When a child is being presented for Baptism, ordinarily the parent(s) or one(s) rightly exercising parental responsibility shall be an active member of the congregation. Those presenting children for Baptism shall promise to provide nurture and guidance within the community of faith until the child is ready to make a personal profession of faith and assume the responsibility of active church membership (W-4.2002, .2003)." The session may also consider a request for the baptism of a child from a Christian parent who is an active member of another congregation. If the session approves such a request, it shall consult the governing body of the other congregation and shall notify them when the Sacrament has been administered (W-2.3014).

Handling requests for baptism using these guidelines is often difficult. If Bob Smith asks that little Bobby be baptized, what is the pastor or the session supposed to do if the parents are not members of their church or any other church? What should they do if Bob's mother calls the pastor and, halfway between tears and outrage, explains that Bob was baptized, confirmed, and married in that very same church? "Just because he hasn't been active in any congregation since he graduated from college in 1990, and because his membership was suspended in his home church, shouldn't make any difference. What's more," the grandmother might add, "if you do not baptize little Bobby, my husband and I are going to withdraw our membership and our sizable pledge!"

What should the session do at this point? Look the other way and baptize Bobby anyway? Decide that "ordinarily" does not apply in this situation? Reinstate Bob's membership as quickly as possible?

Despite the fact that everyone's blood pressure is nearing 200, adopting any of these solutions ignores, of course, the intent of the Directory for Worship. In the *Book of Common Worship* the minister is directed to ask parents, "Relying on God's grace, do you promise to live the Christian faith, and to teach that faith to your child?" The congregation is then asked, "Do you as members of the church of Jesus Christ, promise to guide and nurture

N. and N. by word and deed, with love and prayer, encouraging *them* to know and follow Christ and to be faithful *members* of his church?"

The best way to deal with infant baptism in a case like this may not   be to duck the hard issue or the pain caused to the parents or the grandparents. Yet it is not helpful to be hard-nosed either and simply quote the *Constitution*. The intention of the Directory for Worship is to make sure that the parents of a child about to be baptized are committed to Jesus Christ and determined to bring up their baby in his love. Obviously that is not likely to happen if neither the mother nor the father are members and neither expects to attend church or bring the child to church. Likewise the vows that the members of the church make are designed to ensure that the congregation is serious about its responsibility before God to help the parents in Christian nurture (W-2.3013, G-5.0402a). But they cannot do that without perjuring themselves if the child never comes to church again.

Rather than looking the other way and forcing the parents and church members to make promises they cannot keep, the session and pastors should use this all too "ordinary" situation as one calling for pastoral care and Christian education. When Bob or his mother call, the pastor and session members can set up an appointment with them and explain the theology of infant baptism in the Reformed tradition. They can emphasize that baptism is not "getting little Bobby done" or providing him with some kind of spiritual inoculation. They can also point out that there is no theological reason to be in a hurry to complete the baptism (W-2.3008a). Instead, baptism is a recognition of the fact that the Spirit of God is already at work in his life (W-2.3008b) and that he is loved by God right now and part of the Christian family. It is a visible sign of an invisible grace that will be fully realized only when he later joins the church himself, thus confirming what his mother and father and the congregation did when he was an infant. Bob and his wife can be encouraged to attend church again and be reassured that because the baby cannot be baptized right now is not some kind of punishment. It is merely a short delay until they go through the new member class, rejoin the church, and then have Bobby baptized, at a time that is fully appropriate. Or if the mother and father live in another community, they can go through the process there but still have Bobby baptized later in their home church, having friends and relatives take the vows on behalf of their new church family. In both cases, when the child is baptized, everyone can rejoice and thank God that the meaning of baptism was honored and that all things were done decently and in order.

The Lord's Supper

The Lord's Supper is a celebration of Jesus' death and resurrection, until he comes again. "The Lord's Supper is the sign and seal of eating and drinking in common with the crucified Lord. During his earthly ministry Jesus shared meals with his followers as a sign of community and acceptance and as an occasion for his own ministry. He celebrated Israel's feasts of covenant commemoration" (W-2.4001a).

Although it used to be that Communion could only be performed by ordained ministers (with the assistance of elders and deacons), it has been possible since 1994 for the sacrament to be presented by commissioned lay pastors, under conditions authorized by a presbytery (G-14.0801c(2)). Similarly, in 1999 the General Assembly also began to permit the session or an authorized governing body to allow two or more ordained officers to serve Communion to members isolated from the community's worship (such as people who are shut-in) on the same day it is served to the rest of the congregation (W-3.3616e). The Lord's Supper can also be served at retreats, camps, conferences, and other special gatherings, when authorized by the governing body responsible for the gathering or by the presbytery within whose bounds the event takes place (W-3.6204).

Having considered *who* may serve the Lord's Supper and *where* it may be served, we still might want to ask about its real significance. Another way to put the question is, Why does

Communion differ so much from one celebration to another? Why is it so cheerful one time and so sad another?

An answer can be found in what some call "the many moods of the Lord's Supper." The mood obviously could have something to do with the frame of mind of the pastors and elders serving it, or it could be dependent on the liturgical calendar or the lectionary reading for the day. How we feel about the Lord's Supper will certainly not be the same on Maundy Thursday as it is on the first Sunday of Advent. It will not be the same after a beloved member has died or when a couple has just been married.

But the difference is more profound than that; it has to do with the nature of the sacrament itself. The Lord's Supper has many moods associated with it, and the atmosphere we experience will depend on the theological emphasis we choose for any particular day.

For example, if we concentrate on the fact that the sacrament was instituted by Jesus at a meal given for his disciples on the last day of his life (Mark 14:12–25; Matt. 26:2–29; Luke 22:7–30) and understand from Paul that it is really the *Lord's Supper* (1 Cor. 11:20), then we will concentrate on the Lordship of Jesus Christ. We will also realize that we are his disciples and servants, and that we owe him allegiance above all other people and institutions.

That the supper is the Lord's reminds us that all people who believe in Jesus Christ are welcome at his table. As the Directory for Worship puts it, "All the baptized faithful are to be welcomed at the Table, and none shall be excluded because of race, sex, age, economic status, social class, handicapping condition, difference of culture or language, or any barrier created by human injustice" (W-2.4006).

Not that this openness was always the case in the Reformed tradition. In Calvin's Geneva, a practice was in vogue called "the fencing of the Table" (based loosely on 1 Cor. 10:14–22) that excluded certain people from Communion who were considered morally ineligible to receive it. In Calvin's French liturgy, after the words of institution, the pastor says that if anyone eats the bread or drinks the cup *indignement* (unworthily), he or she will be culpable of the body and the blood of the Lord. Eating or drinking incorrectly, the liturgist intoned, leads to condemnation. Calvin goes on to say that he excommunicates all those who are not in the company of the faithful, especially all idolaters, blasphemers, and heretics, those who destroy the unity of the church.[13]

This practice continued, in one form or another, for a long time in Presbyterian churches in Scotland and in the United States, as members's lives were rigorously scrutinized. People were being excommunicated for such activities as dancing, drinking too much alcohol, or (as one session record put it) singing "lascivious songs."[14] Indeed, in 1764 when John Wesley visited St. Cuthbert's parish church in Edinburgh where Calvin's liturgy was still being observed, he described the process of fencing the table with obvious distaste. As he observed, two tables were set on the sides of the aisles and the minister told the congregation which kind of sinners were forbidden to approach. While the rest of the members received the Lord's Supper, the pastor continued his sermon about the terrible nature of sin, and the whole service sometimes lasted several hours.[15] Presbyterians can be happy that the mood around the table has changed and that even children who are being instructed and nurtured are now welcome at the Lord's Table (G-5.0201, W-2.4011b, 4.2002).[16] We realize that it truly is his table and not ours, that our job is to include people, not exclude them.

Other moods, of course, are also possible when we receive Communion. If we think about the fact that the sacrament is the Lord's *supper*, we gain a different perspective. When friends and families have a meal they pray together, they have a good time, think about the past and look forward to the future. Paul teaches in 1 Corinthians 11:17–34 that the first Christians actually had a meal when they celebrated the Lord's Supper and enjoyed the camaraderie and hospitality of table fellowship. Thus another mood we may assume as we gather around the table is one of "communion," of Christian closeness and fellowship. Paul refers to this as *koinonia,* a sharing of the body of Christ (1 Cor. 10:16–17). Clearly, it is more than merely being with people in a particular place at a particular time: it can also encompass fellowship with Christians all around the world, and with those who have been around the table years earlier, before they passed away.

A third mood that is evident when we gather around the table is connected with Jesus' commandment, "Do this in remembrance of me" (Luke 22:19; 1 Cor. 11:24–25). This atmosphere may be more somber, especially during Lent, because we concentrate on Jesus' suffering, the sacrifice of his death, and the price that our sinfulness costs God. The celebration of the Lord's Supper *in remembrance* leads us to repentance (Mark 1:15). Jesus also related it to God's covenant with the people of Israel. It calls us to remember not only Jesus' death and resurrection but the whole history of the people of faith, all the way back to the exodus and to Abraham.

Another mood of the Lord's Supper, especially when it is linked to Jesus' observance of Passover (see Mark 14:12–16), is one of *victory* and *liberation.* Christians in Third World countries often read the Gospels with very different eyes than ours. They see in Jesus' death and resurrection a fulfillment of his promise to bring good news to the poor, to free the captives, to help the blind see, and to deliver the oppressed (Luke 4:18–19). In the *barrios* of South and Central America and in other parts of the world today, the message of Jesus and his celebration of the Passover on the last day of his life remind them of the exodus and God's promise to deliver the people of God from slavery (Ex. 24:8; Num. 9:5; Deut. 16:1; Heb. 9:20; 11:28). It is possible to attend Communion services in Ethiopia today and hear members testify to how Christ has delivered them from demon possession, or how the church has literally saved their lives from violent attacks or imprisonment when no one else cared. When people share memories of Christ like that there is a tear in every eye.

Another insightful mood we may draw from the Lord's Supper is Jesus' desire to prepare his disciples for the *future reign of God*, in which all things will be done according to the divine will (Mark 14:24–25) and when he will himself be glorified (John 13:31–37). Christians have confidence in things they cannot see, and they hope for things that have not yet happened (Heb. 11:1). A powerful New Testament image connected with the Lord's Supper is that of the eschatological banquet when God will ultimately gather around the table those who have received the call in faith and deserve to be there (Matt. 22:1–14; Luke 14:15–24; Rev. 3:20). Such apocalyptic symbols are always significant to the church at times of change (like the recent turn of the century). But they are always used (often incorrectly) whenever Christians experience hard times or are afraid to look ahead. Since images of the world to come or final judgment are open to misunderstanding, they must be used wisely during Communion.

A final mood that may pervade the Lord's Supper is one of *thanksgiving* and *celebration*. The traditions of the sacrament tell us that Jesus gave thanks (*eucharistēsas;* Matt. 26:27; Mark 14:23; Luke 22:17, 19; 1 Cor. 11:24) before he broke bread and distributed the cup (compare his actions at the feeding of the multitudes, Mark 8:6; Matt. 15:36). That is why its observance is often called the Eucharist, the Feast of Thanksgiving. This mood is particularly evident on Easter or during the Advent season. But it is always an appropriate mood because Christians should be thankful at all times to God for the many gifts they are given, and be willing to express the joy they feel for the forgiveness and empowerment they receive from the living Christ at the table.

The variety of feelings evoked when we join together around Christ's table are derived from the meanings inherent in the sacrament itself. They allow us to encounter a diversity of worship experiences as variegated and rich as the differences of those who gather around the one table, worshiping the one Lord in many different ways, on many different days.

Questions for Study

1. *How often do you think Presbyterians should celebrate Communion? Seven times a year, once a month, once a year?*

2. *When a child is baptized, what are your feelings? Do you wonder what God will call that child to be in the church? Do you think about the significance of your own baptism?*

3. *Do you ever come to the Lord's Table in different frames of mind? How do you receive the Lord's Supper at different times? How do you feel afterward?*

Ministry and Worship in an Interfaith World

"My house shall be called a house of prayer for all peoples" (Isa. 56:7).

In chapter VII of the Directory for Worship there are significant directives to the church about the responsibilities of mission to the world and the need for proclamation and evangelism. God sends the church in the power of the Holy Spirit to announce good news, tell all nations of Christ's call to repentance, proclaim in deed and word that Jesus gave himself to set the world free, and call all people everywhere to believe and follow him as Lord and Savior.

Many occasions, however, call us to go beyond mission and evangelism in our dealings with non-Christians. In one small town a poignant reminder was provided for the whole community to see on the bulletin board in front of the local Baptist church. In essence it said, "We rejoice with our Jewish friends as they celebrate Shavuoth this week." This positive attitude toward neighbors who believe differently than Christians might send Presbyterians scrambling for their religious dictionaries. Shavuoth (the Feast of Weeks) is one of three major Jewish holidays, including Pesach (Passover) and Sukkoth (Festival of Booths). The shortest of their festivals, Shavuoth (Pentecost) is observed fifty days after Passover to celebrate the first harvest and the giving of the Torah to Moses on Mount Sinai.

In many of our communities Christians are faced with a dual role: to be evangelists for Jesus Christ and to live with other firmly established religious groups that are as much a part of our towns and cities as we are. In many areas, clergy groups go beyond normal ecumenical boundaries—they might include the rabbi of a local temple as a full partner in deliberations and plans. In larger areas, interfaith communities might also include Muslims, Hindus, Mormons, Unitarian-Universalists, members of the Baha'i faith, and others.

The *Book of Order* (G-15.0104) says that the Presbyterian Church will seek new opportunities for conversation and understanding with non-Christian religious groups so that interests and concerns may be shared and common actions undertaken where compatible means and aims exist. But the Directory for Worship provides no guidelines for interfaith worship and cooperation. Although prayers of supplication are recommended for nearby churches, state and local communities, the nation, and for people in all kinds of distress, nothing is specifically said about praying for and with people of other faiths (see W-3.3506).[17]

It is difficult enough to decide how to structure worship in ecumenical circles. If the local Roman Catholic church does not invite non-Catholics to receive the Mass, services need to be developed that do not include such elements as will bring offense to other Christian participants. In interfaith worship, developing an order of service is even more challenging. Do we design one that is so generic that no one is offended, or do we insist on the Christian right to pray in Jesus' name, or validate a Jew's desire at the end of the service to ask God to send the Messiah soon? Do we remove our shoes out of respect for Muslim sensitivities? When we have a meal together, do we limit ourselves to vegetarian dishes?

In some local communities, religious organizations have decided not to join together in services that are so general that specific beliefs are never expressed and everyone leaves unfulfilled. Instead, differences are recognized and worshipers are not asked to pretend they do not exist. Worship is carefully designed so it is clear who is leading any particular portion. Each section is explained so that all know why the leaders at that moment are speaking and acting as they are. The background of every scripture or holy text is introduced. Prayers and meditations concentrate on common elements of belief and action: mutual concern for our community's welfare, issues of morality and justice, the need for reconciliation, peacemaking, and openness to one another, and our common belief in one God.

As Presbyterians encounter the world, the need for evangelism always persists. We believe that Jesus Christ is for all people and we want to share the joy of the gospel. Yet people of other religions are likely to be our closest allies and friends in the larger battles we face against violence, prejudice, hatred, secularism, and immorality. How should our worship guidelines reflect the reality of the interfaith world in which we live, while we remain committed to our calling to spread the good news of Jesus Christ?[18]

Questions for Study

1. *Do you have neighbors who are members of other religious groups? How does your church get along with them? Do you work together in the community and worship together?*

2. *What do you know about Muslim or Hindu beliefs? Have you ever been in a Buddhist temple? Have you ever been to another country where Christianity was not the predominant religion? How did you feel about being in the minority?*

Chapter 5

Dealing with Conflict in the Church:
The Rules of Discipline

New Testament Concepts of Discipline

*D*iscipline has been important in the life of the Christian church since its very beginnings. It recognizes that disagreements, problems, and violations of ecclesiastical covenants occur wherever human beings gather as members of institutions. It is in us and in the situation. Believers have always had choices to make. As Psalm 1 reminds us, it is possible to be rooted and growing in God's love and to delight in the law of the Lord, but the choice can also be made to follow the advice of the wicked. Congregations and higher governing bodies in the Presbyterian Church (U.S.A.) cannot choose whether or not conflict and violations will occur on their watch: they can only decide how to respond to them when they inevitably happen. If family members in our own homes have trouble getting along, if cities have rivalries, if politicians use dirty tricks, if nations go to war, it is naive to expect that people are going to get along simply because they are Christians. While it is true that we have high standards as followers of Jesus Christ, we are still redeemed sinners. Sometimes we make mistakes, sometimes we are tempted to do the wrong thing; occasionally we become so hurt or angry that we put our own self-interests first and deliberately try to get our way by injuring other church members or by violating our ordination vows.

Discipline provides a constitutional way to deal with issues in the church when things go wrong and have no obvious way of being solved. According to the opening words of the Rules of Discipline, "Church discipline is the church's exercise of authority given by Christ, both in the direction of guidance, control, and nurture of its members and in the direction of constructive criticism of offenders." This definition is reminiscent of one used in the Presbyterian Church in the United States of America more than fifty years ago: "Discipline is the orderly exercise of that authority, and the application of those principles and laws, which the Church of our Lord Jesus Christ has derived from the Word of God, and has appointed for the instruction, training, and control of its members, officers, congregations, and judicatories."[1]

A key to the principles used to discipline offenders in the early church is found in the teachings of Jesus in Matthew 18:15–35. In a text that may have been modified by a growing church as its administrative concerns became more acute, Jesus urges the *church* (the Greek word in verse 17 is *ekklēsia*) to take careful steps in dealing with those who have injured one another or have violated church order.

The first step is common sense. If a brother (NRSV reads "another member of the church") offends you, "go and point out the fault when the two of you are alone." This principle of dealing with the issue while it still involves only two individuals is a sound one. It keeps the matter private and avoids spreading potential conflict throughout the church. It is always better to deal directly with a problem, rather than hoping it will go away or pretending it does not exist. The church heard similar advice in Ephesians 4:1–3, where the author admonishes church members "to lead a life worthy of the calling to which you have been called, with all humility and gentleness, with patience, bearing with one another in love, making every effort to maintain the unity of the Spirit in the bond of peace." In Romans 12:16–18, Paul urges members not to repay evil for evil, and "if it is possible, so far as it depends on you, live peaceably with all." As Jesus says, the effort to deal with conflict "one-on-one" has a positive effect: "If the member listens to you, you have regained that one."

When private conversation does not solve the problem, Jesus then urges the offended party to take another step and go a second mile. Rather than ignoring the problem or escalating it, Jesus urges us to go back to the person who has done harm, this time in the presence of two or three witnesses. The witnesses provide objectivity and a calming presence. It is much easier to debate or argue when other people are there, because they can help us find a new way of discussing conflicts without merely repeating all the old arguments. They can also give testimony if the conflict escalates.

If the first two steps do not produce positive results, Jesus commands that the one with a grievance should take it to the church courts. In our polity, it would be necessary to file a written statement of an alleged offense (along with supporting evidence) with the clerk of a session, presbytery, synod, or the General Assembly in order to request disciplinary action (D-10.0100). If even that kind of activity brings no satisfaction, Jesus suggests that the offended party should ignore the other person altogether (Matt. 18:17).

We see from this teaching that the main purpose of discipline is to resolve differences and restore members who have violated church order back to the church. Paul calls for the same outcome in Galatians 6:1–2 when he writes, "My friends, if anyone is detected in a transgression, you who have received the Spirit should restore such a one in a spirit of gentleness. Take care that you yourselves are not tempted. Bear one another's burdens, and in this way you will fulfill the law of Christ." The book of James views church discipline in an even more sober light: bringing a wandering sinner back to the church will save him or her from spiritual death and cover a multitude of sins (James 5:19–20).

Other passages in the New Testament demonstrate that later believers continued to find it difficult to resolve conflict or to bypass the necessity of having church bodies intervene in church disputes. In Acts 15 we encounter an ecclesiastical controversy so severe that it threatened to fracture the new church. The issue was, should Gentiles be circumcised or not? Acts 15:1–2 seems to minimize the conflict involved:

> Certain individuals came down from Judea and were teaching the brothers, "unless you are circumcised according to the custom of Moses, you cannot be saved." And after Paul and Barnabas had no small dissension and debate with them, Paul and Barnabas and some of the others were appointed to go up to Jerusalem to discuss this question with the apostles and elders.

The Greek text translated "had no small discussion and debate" clearly indicates that the argument was red hot and that those involved were really very angry at each other. Only after careful debate and a determination by the body to listen to each other (v. 12) was it decided, somewhat in a spirit of compromise, that Gentiles did not have to abide by Jewish purity laws, with four exceptions (v. 29). Yet according to Paul, the debate continued (depending upon the interpretation given to Galatians 2), and even though the church resolutions were all in order, Jewish members still discriminated against Gentiles. Paul had a face-to-face confrontation with Peter, James, and others in Antioch over the same issue (Gal. 2:11–21). Paul was so angry that he hoped those who continued to mislead the church on this matter and insist on circumcision would slip and mutilate themselves. Disgusted, he desired that they should not aggravate him or the church anymore (Gal. 5:11–12; 6:17).

Additional issues created conflict in the early church. One group successfully provoked the Galatians to follow "another gospel" than the one that Paul preached (Gal. 1:6–9), and he had to urge his readers to return to the truth. Philemon and his slave had a strong difference of opinion about slavery and Paul had to mediate their differences. Paul sent Onesimus back home, hoping that a new relationship would be created based on commonality in Christ (the letter to Philemon). First Timothy indicates that internal conflicts continued to plague the church, so much so that the author had to urge members not to accept accusations against elders unless they had the evidence of two or three witnesses (5:19). Although he instructs those in charge that the ones who continue to sin should be rebuked publicly ("in the presence of all," v. 20), he reminds them before God that the whole matter must be handled without prejudice (the Greek *prokrima* means "prejudgment, discrimination," v. 21). They must do nothing on the basis of partiality (*prosklisis*, partisanship, political favoritism). In one of the final books of the New Testament we learn that a man named Diotrephes was so convinced that he was number one in the church that he ignored the authority of John, not only spreading false charges about him, but refusing to accept his emissaries and removing others from the church who did want to meet with them (3 John 9).

Reformation Principles of Discipline

As Presbyterians we receive our guidelines about proper conduct in times of trouble in the church not only from the writings of the New Testament but from the writings of the Reformers of the sixteenth century. Since John Knox was influenced by John Calvin in the formulation of the *First Book of Discipline* of the Church of Scotland in 1560, it is useful to see what Calvin has to teach us about church discipline.

According to Calvin, discipline is essential to the life of the church. "If no society, indeed, no house which has even a small family, can be kept in proper condition without discipline, it is much more necessary in the church, whose condition should be as ordered as possible."[2]

Discipline, he contends, serves like a bridle on a spirited horse, "to restrain and tame those who rage against the doctrine of Christ; or like a spur to arouse those of little inclination; and also sometimes like a father's rod to chastise mildly and with the gentleness of Christ's Spirit those who have more seriously lapsed."[3]

Following the teaching of Jesus in Matthew 18:15–20, Calvin urges members who have grievances with each other to deal with them one-on-one. Major reasons why individuals might be admonished include refusal to perform their duty willingly, insolent behavior, dishonorable living, and performing an act that is blameworthy.[4]

Calvin gives the major reasons for church discipline: to preserve the integrity of the Lord's Supper, to prevent good being corrupted by the constant corruption of the wicked, and to overcome the shame of those who are at fault so they may be urged to repent.[5]

Following 1 Timothy 5, Calvin also urges the church to avoid partiality. In his view, no members should be exempt from ecclesiastical discipline. All crowns and scepters must submit to Christ, and the church does not have the right to look the other way or cut deals just because an offender is a well-known pastor, a wealthy donor, or a government official.

> For great kings ought not to count it any dishonor to prostrate themselves as suppliants before Christ, the King of Kings; nor ought they to be displeased that they are judged by the church. For inasmuch as they hear almost nothing but mere flatteries in their courts, it is all the more necessary for them to be rebuked by the Lord through the mouth of priests. Rather, they ought to desire not to be spared by the priests, that God may spare them.[6]

Howard Rice points out that Calvin was responsible for reviving the concept of church discipline at a time when it had almost disappeared. What is more, he intertwined it with the concept of pastoral care so that in most cases the offender could be admonished and restored in a spirit of gentleness and love (after proper confession of guilt).[7] Rice says Calvin took people seriously enough to point out problems, warn them of dangers, and call them to account. If he exercised severe discipline at times in Geneva, it was to try to bring members to repentance, and, if possible, with a spirit of moderation. In Rice's opinion, modern Christians are so afraid of offending other church members that we neglect to care for them at all. "The rigorous form of discipline that took place in Geneva during Calvin's tenure was for the purpose of repentance rather than punishment, and it was not intended to be undertaken without remorse and self-examination on the part of those passing judgment."[8]

Questions for Study

1. *What does your congregation do if members disrupt the peace and unity of the church? Do you ignore their behavior and hope that it will go away? Do church officers confront them and ask for different behavior?*
2. *Can you think of instances in which church officers should be removed? Should church members be allowed to remain as members if they gossip about other members or tell lies? Should their membership be continued if their behavior is flagrantly unethical?*
3. *Would your session have the courage to tell members that their behavior is contrary to what is expected in your church?*

Discipline in the Twenty-first Century Church

The need for church discipline and its advantages are obvious. James Angell is poetic in his recitation of its value.

> Discipline is strength.
> It eradicates confusion, minimizes injustice.
> It prevents controlling majorities from ignoring unpopular minorities. . . .
> Discipline is the servant of mission.
> And the friend of sacrifice.
> In spite of its negative, woodshed kind of sound, it is part of a *positive* obedience to Jesus Christ.[9]

On the other hand, it is not difficult to see how reliance on church discipline could damage personal relationships, or how the excessive use of the strategies of polity could replace prayer and honest theological debate to settle disputes. Writing in the

1953 edition of *Presbyterian Law for the Local Church*, Eugene Carson Blake warns that no law or manual can prevent trouble or sharp division in the church. Problems occur because people fail to listen to the Spirit or because they use the church's law solely to gain a victory over others. The correct way to resolve differences is not to take sides on an issue but to find enough people who are willing to seek the guidance of God under the direction of the laws of the church. What is needed is people who are willing to listen to others with whom they have differences and who agree to abide by the decision of the church, once it is made. Blake reminds us that provisions for complaint and appeal exist for those who are still convinced that a certain action is wrong or runs contrary to their conscience, and they may use those methods, rather than others that rely on rancor and mistrust. Before beginning such a process, he warns, all members need to examine their own hearts and the purity of their motives, and pray to God for guidance.[10]

Forty years later, the 205th General Assembly (1993) took up the same refrain, warning that even though the *Book of Order* reflects how Presbyterians understand faith and order, it cannot be the primary unifying document for our denomination. In other words, church unity is not easily achieved if we concentrate primarily on the processes of amendment, church discipline, and *Robert's Rules of Order* to decide who we are and who we are going to be.[11] In order to move into the future, Presbyterians are admonished to make sure that our theology and polity are continually subject to the principles of reformation by the Word of God, under the guidance of the Holy Spirit. We are encouraged to make sure that the *Book of Order* delineates the broad principles of Presbyterian polity without turning it into a manual of operations.[12] "We are persuaded that the future of the PC(USA) will not be found in amendments to the *Book of Order*. Governance in the Reformed tradition is not a foremost adherence to a set of procedures; it is the constant struggle to be faithful to the God who called the church into being and whose spirit reforms the church when it is able to hear and respond."[13]

More recently, concerns have also been raised by the Office of the Stated Clerk along similar lines. In a policy reflection published on *OGA Online*,[14] the Department of Constitutional Services discusses the issue raised when church members or governing bodies sign or endorse covenants of dissent against certain provisions of the *Book of Order*, or support the withholding of per capita contributions as a means of protest. Observing that there is a difference between dissent and a stated intent to violate the *Constitution*, the article warns that members could be liable to administrative review or judicial process if they go beyond dissent to advocating change through unconstitutional means.

At the end of the study it is noted that in the Rules of Discipline "judicial process is not the primary or preferred method for Christians to work out their disagreements."[15] Even though charges might be brought against those who sign covenants of dissent (particularly against constitutional restrictions of the ordination of gays and lesbians) or the withholding of per capita contributions, the Stated Clerk and the Department of Constitutional Services have not advocated the use of such a method to address conflicting views. "While such actions may be possible, we fear that they may also be destructive to our covenant commitment to seek truth and faithfulness together in our Lord Jesus Christ."[16]

As the memorandum from the Office of the Stated Clerk points out, the Rules of Discipline themselves make it clear that judicial process is not the best method of settling disputes or differences of opinion. In fact, this part of the *Constitution* should really be used as a means of last resort, after all other efforts have failed. "The traditional biblical obligation to conciliate, mediate, and adjust differences without strife is not diminished by these Rules. . . . The biblical duty of church people to 'come to terms quickly with your accuser while you are on the way to court . . .' (Matthew 5:25) is not abated or diminished. It remains the duty of every church member to try (prayerfully and seriously) to bring about an adjustment or settlement of the quarrel, complaint, delinquency, or irregularity asserted, and to avoid formal proceedings under the Rules of Discipline unless, after prayerful deliberation, they are determined to be necessary to preserve the purity and purposes of the church" (D-1.0103). Not that this directive is easy to carry out. Despite the number of studies that have been provided by our denomination and other bodies concerning ways to resolve conflict,[17] it is still difficult for most individuals and sessions to deal with intense disagreement when it strikes their own congregations. Consider cases close to home. How does your church deal with conflict? How do you respond if there are personality differences that disrupt your life together? How does the session react when severe disagreements crop up about important decisions that have to be made?

Many times our tendency is to ignore the conflict and hope that it will go away. Or we adopt the posture of "fight or flight." Or our first instinct is to defend our positions. Or we try to force dissenters out. Or we decide to quit ourselves because we cannot stand the pain of a church in so much tension.

Another response is to take a pastoral approach when members overtly or covertly challenge decisions made by the session and the pastor(s). Rather than ignoring the complaints or becoming defensive, the pastors and elders can take the "high road," no matter how unfair the charges are, and work to reduce anxiety and tension. They can adopt what Edwin H. Friedman calls a "nonanxious presence."[18] Rather than overreacting, they might call the concerned members, ask if they could come over and visit them and listen to their complaints and work for genuine understanding. Even if policies cannot be changed, they can be carefully explained so the members will at least know they have been heard.

This approach to disagreement is often more difficult and more painful than other alternatives, but is also more biblical and spiritual. It is in keeping with the teaching of Jesus that advises his followers to go directly to a brother or sister in a time of trouble (Matt. 18:15–20). Jesus knows we will have opponents and even enemies, but he commands us to make our first response one of love (Matt. 5:44; see Rom. 12:20; Prov. 25:21–22) and to settle matters quickly with accusers, rather than letting conflicts fester (Matt. 5:25).

If sessions cannot settle matters themselves, it is possible to take additional steps by asking presbytery's Committee on Ministry to help, either by requesting an outsider to observe the process and make suggestions, or by consulting an independent mediator.

Meditation services exist in most large cities and are used by government agencies, nonprofit institutions, universities and colleges, and industries to settle seemingly irreconcilable differences. Mediation can take the edge off a conflict. By allowing people to sit down at the same table and slowly and methodically prepare guidelines for future discussions, and by carefully examining the issues that divide the body, real progress can be made. Although it is not possible to determine beforehand what the issues of contention might be in a particular church, the principles of active listening, negotiation, and compromise usually help defuse situations that could disable a congregation for years to come. (See the provisions for mediation recommended in G-9.0600.)

Questions for Study

1. *Do you think your session would call on mediators if issues that divide you could not be sorted out?*
2. *Which takes more courage, to let conflicting issues slide or to confront them directly?*
3. *Do members of your church know how to fight fairly?*

Using the Rules of Discipline

When other methods of settling disputes fail, Presbyterians are fortunate to have a tested judicial process that can be used by the Holy Spirit to solve problems and discipline those who have abused their power.

The current Rules of Discipline were adopted by the General Assembly in 1995 and implemented on July 6, 1996. Prior to that, the reuniting church followed revised policies used in the two joining churches since 1983. Before reunion, the Presbyterian Church in the United States of America referred to this section of the *Constitution* as the Book of Discipline.

The purposes of church discipline are clearly laid out in the first section of the Rules of Discipline.

- To honor God by making clear the significance of membership in the body of Christ. The first assumption is that being a member of the Presbyterian church means something and requires adherence to definite standards if one is to continue to serve as a responsible officer.
- To preserve the purity of the church by nourishing the individual within the life of the believing community.
- To correct or restrain wrongdoing.
- To restore the unity of the church by removing the causes of discord and division.
- To secure the just, speedy, and economical determination of the proceedings. Since Presbyterians believe in gospel and law, the church makes sure that charges are brought and heard according to fair legal practices and that they do not drag out for an inordinate time. It is also important to make sure that trials do not continue for a long time for another reason: often accusers and defendants both must retain attorneys versed in Presbyterian constitutional law, and their fees and the cost of preparing evidence and calling witnesses can be very expensive. In one recent case in which charges were brought against a pastor for sexual abuse, a presbytery spent over $30,000 in legal and other fees before the case was settled just minutes before the permanent judicial commission was scheduled to begin hearing it.

What is the purpose of discipline in the Presbyterian church? According to D-1.0102, in keeping with the biblical and reformed principles mentioned earlier, it is to build up the church, rather than destroy it; for redemption, rather than punishment; and for the dispensation of mercy so that the Great Ends of the Church (G-1.0200) may be achieved. Judicial process is implemented primarily within the context of pastoral care and oversight, not for making offenders pay for violations of the *Constitution*.

Cases can only be heard by four bodies within the church: the session, and the permanent judicial commissions of presbyteries, synods, and the General Assembly (see D-3.0101, 5.0000).

Two types of cases may be heard. (1) A *remedial* case is one in which a lower governing body—the General Assembly Council or an entity of the General Assembly—is charged with an *irregularity* (an erroneous decision or action) or a *delinquency* (an omission or a failure to act). (2) A *disciplinary* case is one in which a church member or officer is charged with an offense (D-2.0203a); an offense being defined as "any act or omission by a member or officer of the church that is contrary to the Scriptures or the *Constitution*" (D-2.0203). Remembering that the *Constitution* consists of the *Book of Order* and the *Book of Confessions*, it is clear that disciplinary charges could involve violations of any provisions of the Form of Government (like the vows that officers and members take), the Directory for Worship (failing to observe Reformed practices of worship), or the injunctions of the various Reformed confessions. Although it is difficult to ascertain precisely how one could be censured for violating the latter, since the confessions span a wide time range and do not all teach the same thing, they all contain references to Scripture in general and some refer to the Ten Commandments in particular. Thus it is possible to imagine how unethical conduct could be conceived to be in violation of Part I of the *Constitution* (see the discussion below in chapter 8, "Professional and Ethical Standards for Church Officers").

All charges above a session level are heard by the permanent judicial commission of the appropriate governing body. And since our system of justice works somewhat like the court system in the nation (local, state, and federal), appeals can be made until they reach the Permanent Judicial Commission of the General Assembly, the final court of appeal in the church (D-5.0000).

Concerns about violations of the *Constitution* do not always have to go through the courts of the church. Whenever a member of the body feels personally aggrieved or is convinced that the governing body involved made a faulty decision, he or she can file a *dissent* or a *protest* with the body. A *dissent* is a verbal statement made on the floor of the meeting in question, in which the member declares disagreement with an action just passed and asks that his or her name be recorded in opposition (G-9.0303). A *protest* is a written statement, filed with the clerk or stated clerk before the adjournment of a particular meeting. "If a protest is expressed in decorous and respectful language, the governing body shall enter it in its minutes in recognition of the person's right of conscience" (G-9.0304).

A *complaint*, on the other hand, is a more formal way of registering opposition. It is to be used only after careful consideration, because it leads to more drastic and time-consuming actions. The complaint is a written statement alleging an irregularity in an action or a delinquency (D-6.0102). It may lead to a stay of enforcement (a delay in implementation of an approved action by the body, D-6.0103) and the hearing of the charges before the appropriate permanent judicial commission. Procedures for filing a complaint are carefully laid out in the Rules of Discipline (D-6.0200). Appropriate forms to use in all aspects of judicial processes (fifty-one of them) are provided in an appendix following D-14.0000.

The results of trials differ, depending on the kind of case that is heard. In a remedial case, if a complaint against a governing body is not sustained, the action will stand as approved by that body. If parts or all of the charges are sustained, the permanent judicial commission will order an appropriate action or direct the lower governing body to reconsider the matter (D-7.0402).

In a disciplinary case against a member or officer, five different judgments may be reached. If the decision is for *acquittal*, the defendant is declared innocent. If the permanent judicial commission pronounces a judgment of *rebuke* (the least severe degree of church censure), the character of the offense and an admonition are set forth publicly (D-12.0102).

A second form of censure, one that was just included in the Rules of Discipline in 1997, consists not only of declaring the offense and providing a public rebuke; it also mandates a period of supervised rehabilitation (D-12.0103). The purpose of this censure is to make sure the offender receives professional guidance and counseling, which may include psychological or psychiatric evaluation. Although the offender may continue in office, he or she can only do so while receiving the required supervision and help.

The third and fourth levels of censure are more severe since they include *temporary exclusion from ordained office* (D-12.0104) and *removal from office or membership* (D-12.0105). Temporary removal for a definite period of time is imposed for a more aggravated offense and requires the completion of a time of supervised rehabilitation. During that time, the person censured cannot participate in any function of ordained office, or participate or vote in any meetings. If a pastor is found guilty, his or her pastoral relationship with a congregation is dissolved. Permanent removal, as the term implies, involves the setting aside of the ordination and election of the guilty party and requires removal from all offices (with or without the removal of church membership, in the case of an elder or deacon). In both cases, the person judged to be guilty can be restored by the governing body applying the censure, if it is fully satisfied that the action is justified and if the person makes a reaffirmation of faith (in the case of an elder or deacon) or is reordained (for pastors). In such cases, the moderator of the governing body shall declare that repentance has been made and a restoration to membership and/or a full service of ordination shall take place to restore the elder, deacon, or pastor back to office (D-12.0200).

One offense that will continue to be of major concern in the twenty-first century will no doubt be that of sexual misconduct. When ministers apply for positions in the church, they must sign a form attached to their "Personal Information Form" in which they certify one of two things: (1) that no civil, criminal, or ecclesiastical complaint has ever been sustained or is pending against them, and (2) that they have never resigned or been terminated from a position for reasons related to sexual conduct; or that they cannot make the above certification (followed by explanatory comments). Most presbyteries provide manuals for pastors, elders, employees, and volunteers that include sexual misconduct policies, procedures for disciplinary or nondisciplinary cases (usually based on General Assembly guidelines), and definitions of terms like "sexual harassment," "sexual abuse/ malfeasance," and "child sexual abuse." Sexual abuse is taken so seriously in the Rules of Discipline that it is the only offense for which charges may be made later than three years from the time of the commission of the alleged offense. (See D-10.0401 and further discussion below in chapter 8, "Professional and Ethical Standards for Church Officers.")

Although it is rare that conflict reaches the point in Presbyterian governing bodies that charges must be brought and trials conducted, it happens often enough to remind us that a fair and just system of legal redress exists in our church to ensure the preservation of our faith and traditions, and to prevent people from holding office who have violated their confession as followers of Jesus Christ and their ordination vows as officers or pastors in the Presbyterian Church (U.S.A.).[19] As the 205th General Assembly (1993) declared, "Presbyterian polity recognizes the sovereignty of God, which makes all authority subordinate to God's authority and the object of God's judgment and grace. . . . It testifies to the oneness of the church through the interrelatedness of its governing bodies. While providing for liberty of conscience, there has been an orderly process for protecting that liberty while seeking the will of God together in gathered assemblies."[20]

Questions for Study

1. *Does your congregation have sexual misconduct guidelines for staff and volunteers? Do you have guidelines for church school teachers and youth leaders about the proper way to deal with children? Does your school, scout troop, or athletic team have guidelines for the proper behavior of adult leaders?*

2. *Read two disciplinary cases that were brought before the General Assembly in the last year (found in the* Minutes of the General Assembly, *Part I,* Journal*). Can you understand the issues involved? Do you agree with the verdicts?*

Chapter 6

The *Book of Confessions*:
A Thumbnail Sketch

Introduction

During recent years, Presbyterians have been turning to the *Book of Confessions* with renewed interest. As they have considered several controversial amendments to the *Constitution* on fidelity and chastity and have debated whether or not gays and lesbians should be ordained as elders, deacons, and pastors, many members have wondered about the purpose of the *Book of Confessions*, its origins and function, and how it should be properly used by the church.

In the Greek New Testament, the verb "confess" (*homologeō*), as it applies to statements of belief, means "to say the same thing," "to declare publicly," "to acknowledge." Paul says that every tongue should confess that Jesus is Lord, to the glory of God (Phil. 2:11). In 1 Timothy 6:12 we read about "the good confession" which is made in the presence of many witnesses (also see Rom, 10:10; 2 Cor. 9:13; Heb. 4:14; 10:23; 1 John 2:23; 4:3, etc.). These confessions are similar to the great creedal statements of the Old Testament in which the people expressed their belief in one God and one God alone, and vowed to worship with their whole heart, soul, and might (Deut. 6:4).

The Presbyterian Church (U.S.A.) uses the *Book of Confessions* to declare to its members and the world who and what it is, what it believes, and what it resolves to do. "These statements identify the church as a community of people known by its convictions as well as by its actions. They guide the church in its study and interpretation of the Scriptures; they summarize the essence of Christian tradition; they direct the church in maintaining sound doctrines; they equip the church for its work of proclamation" (G-2.0100b).

Contrary to what is often assumed, the first book of confessions was not put together in 1967 when the Confession of 1967 was adopted and combined with eight other historic statements of the Reformed faith ("A Brief Statement of Faith" was added in 1991). As Arthur Cochrane points out, between 1523 and 1566 at least twelve different confessions were written by various Reformed churches, and in 1581 a collection or *Harmonia* was published as a temporary substitute for a union document.[1] Prior to that, in 1572, the General Assembly in Scotland accepted the Second Helvetic Confession, Calvin's Catechism, and the Heidelberg Catechism as suitable faith statements to stand with the Scots Confession of 1560.[2]

Professor Edward Dowey of Princeton Theological Seminary, who was the chairperson of the 1967 committee, summarizes the five reasons why a new *Book of Confessions* was presented to the church. (1) It places our actual history and doctrinal tradition before our eyes in a way no single confession, old or new, can do. (2) The *Book of Confessions* makes clear the actual nature of the creeds and confessions: how they appear irregularly in response to various needs of the church. They show how the Christian faith lives and moves in history. (3) The older and newer creeds and confessions give perspective on the thought, worship, and ethics of the church, which is important in our quickly changing world. (4) The ecumenical age will mature more quickly when each tradition knows its own unity and variety. (5) The *Book of Confessions* gives the church the freedom and courage to respond to new occasions, while it is being strengthened by the examples of Christians who have gone before.[3]

Confessions are necessarily dated and are expressed in the language of a particular place and time. They are, as John Leith says, "datable in a particular history." Sometimes it is sufficient to say that "Jesus is Lord"; sometimes it is necessary to focus on the relationship between God and the Son, or on the authority of the Bible, or (as the focus has been in recent years) on the question of ordination and personal sexual ethics.[4]

As valuable as the *Book of Confessions* is to the ongoing definition of doctrine, our *Constitution* reminds us that confessions are not primary sources of faith and action. "These confessional statements are subordinate standards in the church, subject to the authority of Jesus Christ, the Word of God, as the Scriptures bear witness to him" (G-2.0200). As Donald McKim points out in his careful study of confessional history, confessions have a "provisional authority" because they are the work of limited, fallible human beings and churches (and are therefore open to change and amendment; see G-2.0200, 18.0000). They have a "temporal authority" because the expression of faith in a living God must always be open to the ongoing work of Christ and the intervention of the Spirit. They have a "relative authority" because they are subordinate to the higher authority of Scripture, which is always the norm in Reformed churches for discovering the work and will of God in every time and place.[5]

During the next few years, as Presbyterians explore the ethical guidelines for Christian living as found in the *Book of Confessions*, it will be important to remember that what they profess and teach will always be subject to a correct interpretation of Scripture. Even more significantly, we must remember that for us the chief and final arbiter of faith and practice is not the confessions, or even the Bible, but the witness of the living Christ, the Word of God made flesh. Any determination we make must stand under the scrutiny of his judgment, love, and passion for justice. And we will need to submit every decision to a prayerful consideration of what he would have done and would have us do. "All ministry in the church is a gift from Jesus Christ. Members and officers alike serve mutually under the mandate of

Christ who is the chief minister of all. His ministry is the basis of all ministries" (G-6.0101). As Edward Dowey puts it, "The church must have institutional structures, but not one of them—creed, pastoral office, sacramental tradition, administrative provisions—can usurp the role of Christ, who is the sole bond of union in the church catholic."[6]

Questions for Study

1. *What does it mean to say that the confessions "identify the church as a community of people known by its convictions as well as by its actions" (G-2.0100b)?*
2. *In what sense does the* Book of Confessions *demonstrate that Presbyterians give witness to the faith of the Church catholic (G-2.0300)?*

A Brief Statement of Faith (1991)

In the search to understand the purpose and use of the *Book of Confessions*, we begin with two confessions written during the lifetime of many of today's Presbyterians. If confessions express the faith of believers as they respond to new occasions in light of historic statements of Christian tradition, it will be helpful to see what Presbyterians have said most recently about what we believe and how we intend to act.

A Brief Statement of Faith was adopted by the General Assembly in 1991 after a long process of study, writing, and editing. As a result of the reunion of the two branches of the Presbyterian Church in 1983, Moderator J. Randolph Taylor appointed twenty people to serve on a special committee to prepare a brief statement of the Reformed faith that, in its final form, could be read quickly and used by congregations in services of worship. It was designed to show that, despite our diversity, Presbyterians are one in faith and mission.[7]

This confession differed from its predecessors in a number of significant ways:

- It put a strong emphasis on the earthly ministry of Jesus and his role in human suffering (reflecting interest in Liberation Theology), rather than concentrating on his eternal origins and nature.
- It made it clear that both women and men are called to ministry, repudiating the idea in earlier confessions that only men may serve.
- A strong emphasis (reflecting eco-justice concerns) was placed on God's creation, confessing our tendency to exploit the beauty of the earth.
- In reference to the Trinity, the Brief Statement uses more inclusive, gender-neutral language to describe God, although the doxology added as a final sentence returns to traditional categories of Father, Son, and Spirit.[8]
- The confession concludes with a strong statement about the role of the Holy Spirit in the worship, daily tasks, mission, and ecumenical work of the church as it strives to unmask idolatries in culture and to labor for justice, freedom, and peace.

Questions for Study

1. *In lines 49–51, the Brief Statement refers to God as a "nurse" and as a father welcoming a prodigal home. Look up in the cross-reference appendix those scriptures and references in the confessions that validate using varied language to speak of God.*

2. *What is the significance of emphasizing (in the first and last sections) that nothing in life or in death can separate us from the love of God?*

The Confession of 1967

Work on the Confession of 1967 began in 1956, when the Presbytery of Amarillo sent an overture to the General Assembly requesting a rewording of the Westminster Shorter Catechism, a document used in many churches as a primary teaching tool in confirmation classes. A special committee was eventually appointed and chaired by Professor Edward Dowey of Princeton Theological Seminary for the purpose of writing a brief, contemporary statement of faith.

Based on the theme of reconciliation found in 2 Corinthians 5:17, this confession may be visualized as a cross. On a horizontal plane, it spoke to Americans separated by many barriers. At a time when racial, sexual, and economic differences divided some communities and the nation as a whole struggled painfully with issues about the morality of the Vietnam War, the confession called for reconcilation of neighbors and enemies in the name of Christ. The vertical arm focused on reconciliation with God, particularly on faith in the person and work of Jesus Christ, and on the forgiveness only he can bring.

A second major emphasis, on the nature and purpose of the Bible (C-9.27ff.), was fiercely debated prior to adoption, as Presbyterians struggled to express their belief that, although the words of the Old and New Testaments were influenced by the life, history, and culture of the people who wrote them, they still contain the Word of God for us, especially as that Word is revealed in the Word made flesh, Jesus Christ our Lord.

Because I was a student at Princeton Seminary at the time, I remember vividly both the excitement and the anxiety created in the church by the proposed confession. Some charged that it threatened Presbyterian tradition by abandoning the Westminster Standards relied on since the seventeenth century, and they seized on the proposed changes as unfaithful, irreverent, and heretical. Members of the committee were often harassed from every side and were sometimes even accused of being Communists.

For others of us, however, the discussion and debate brought a fresh breeze of the Spirit, allowing us at last to say what we really believed and felt. Freed from the strictness, theological reserve, and archaic language of Westminster, we spent hours in the classrooms, in dorms late at night, and in churches that we visited with the Princeton Choir, trying to understand the meaning and purpose of Scripture, debating the centrality of Christ in the church, and exploring the work of Calvin and other

Reformers in the light of the work of Karl Barth, Emil Brunner, Rudolf Bultmann, Dietrich Bonhoeffer, Paul Tillich, and others. This experience reminds the church how invigorating the process of writing a new confession can be. And it illustrates why, for many Presbyterians today, the Confession of 1967 remains the most significant confession in our tradition, and how in many ways it still provides the confessional guidelines we need for the discussions and debates that engage us now.

The Confession of 1967 is outstanding in many aspects. Rather than focusing primarily on Christian doctrine, it begins by calling Presbyterians to make certain that they provide a present witness to Jesus Christ in the world in which they live (C-9.01). As the Preface puts it, "The purpose of the Confession of 1967 is to call the church to that unity in confession and mission which is required of disciples today" (C-9.05). Its authors and many of those who would later use it had passed through World War II and the period of the Holocaust and were presently agonizing over the U.S. role in Vietnam, while the world was still living under the very real threat of nuclear annihilation. Consequently, the Confession of 1967 refuses to identify the Christian life with the sovereignty of any one nation (C-9.45). At a time when national security was a mantra of political philosophy, this new statement of faith boldly declared that the church must search for forgiveness of enemies and for peace "even at risk to national security" (C-9.45). Although that calling creates difficult demands, Presbyterians proclaimed that they would pursue it with a sense of urgency and hope, striving for a new world, depending on the ultimate power of God (C-9.55).

A church that had relied on the Westminster Standards since 1647 now vigorously examined its faith in the light of modern principles of biblical criticism. It saw itself as a agent for peace in the international sphere and looked with deep concern at the problems of urbanization and prejudice and called for reconciliation at all levels of life.

As Edward Dowey says, the new confession was designed to express the faith of Presbyterians, not just for that moment in time, but for many years to come. "The Confession of 1967 is, I think, still far ahead of the church, rather than something that it has now used and gotten beyond. It's in many ways a simple looking document, but it is very—what would you say—it's very muscular. It rewards study. It can lead us for an indefinite future time."[9]

Questions for Study

1. *In what sense is the Bible the witness without parallel to God, if it reflects the life, culture, and history of its writers?*
2. *Are there any social or ethical issues which the church must address that are being ignored today (C-9.43–47)? Are there any that will be particularly important in the coming years? Are there any that are not included in this confession?*

The Theological Declaration of Barmen

In 1937 Dr. Otto Dibelius, a general superintendent in the Prussian Evangelical Church, and the Rev. Martin Niemöller, a pastor in Berlin, published a pamphlet titled *Wir rufen Deutschland zu Gott* (We are calling Germany to God). On the frontispiece they reminded Germans that above all they must stand before God. Whoever knows this, they wrote, must say it, for in this hour of decision nothing else can be expected. "With such an attitude is this booklet written. Let him hear, who is able! And God help Germany!"

In 1934 Lutheran, Reformed, and United church pastors and lay leaders responded with similar intensity and courage to the atrocities of the Third Reich when they met in Barmen-Wuppertal, May 29–31. The resulting declaration, largely written by Karl Barth, called Christians to oppose Hitler's attempt to destroy the church and make it a puppet of fascism.

In a few short years the Nazis had caused immense damage. Hitler had already established the Reich Church with Ludwig Müller as its bishop and he was working to destroy the political power of the Roman Catholic Church through his concordat with the Holy See. Quickly the Nazis dismantled any remaining vestiges of democracy in Germany and began systematic terrorism against the Jews.[10]

The Jews were not the only victims of Nazi racism and prejudice, even though their destruction was the Reich's most nefarious and bloodthirsty goal. Starting with small fringe groups, a Gestapo order of December 1938 made it clear that it was also intended to destroy many Christian groups. This list included the names of forty-one organizations, including the International Jehovah's Witnesses, God's Social Parish, the Anabaptist sect, and various Seventh Day Adventist groups, among others.

We are still shocked to see photos that show how deeply Naziism had penetrated remaining churches: Nazi altars with portraits of Hitler in the center and babies waiting to be baptized in front of paraments festooned with the swastika.[11]

Regardless of the content of Nazi agreements with churches or what was said in public, Hitler had his own opinion about the future. In December of 1941 he reportedly said, "The war will be over one day. I shall then consider that my life's final task will be to solve the religious problem. Only then will the State of the German nation be guaranteed once and for all. . . . The organized lie must be smashed. . . . The final state must be: in the pulpit, a senile officiant; facing him, a few sinister old women, as gaga and as poor in spirit as anyone could wish." Another time he was equally belligerent. "Do you really believe the masses will ever be Christian again? Nonsense! Never again. That tale is finished. No one will listen to it again. But we can hasten matters. The parsons will be made to dig their own graves. They will betray their God to us. They will betray anything for the sake of their miserable little jobs and incomes."[12]

The Barmen Declaration indicates that many of the pastors and laymen (including one woman, Stephanie von Mackensen) courageously confessed that they were not going to let Hitler become their leader or their god. Even those who do not read German can sense their determination in section 4 (8.21). "We reject the false doctrine, as though the Church, apart from this ministry, could and were permitted to give to itself, or allow to be given to it, special leaders [*ausgestattete Führer*] vested with ruling powers."

Although some later criticized the Declaration for not going far enough (it never specifically speaks out against racist policies against the Jews), this confession still provides a powerful warning today to those who want to accommodate the message of Christ to any state or federal policy. It warns us against the danger of maintaining silence when minority groups, immigrants, or the poor are officially discriminated against. It warns us about settling for temporary power and prestige in the face of God's eternal kingdom. Today it still calls all Christians to God, and as the Confession of 1967 reminds us, "Although nations may serve God's purposes in history, the church which identifies the sovereignty of any one nation or any one way of life with the cause of God denies the Lordship of Christ and betrays its calling" (9.45).[13]

Questions for Study

1. *If you knew that you might be sent to a concentration camp if you expressed your faith as a Christian, would you be able to sign a document like the Declaration of Barmen?*

2. *What happens to the church and to the world if followers of Jesus Christ are afraid to speak out against injustice in every age?*

The Westminster Standards

The Westminster Standards, written between 1643 and 1647, served as the foundation of the theology and practice of Presbyterians, Congregationalists, and Baptists for nearly three hundred and twenty years. Used as guidelines for church order, for the exploration of the Christian faith in a world increasingly embracing the scientific method, for ethical direction, for worship, for instruction of adult converts and children, few theological works have contributed as consistently to the power and spirit of Protestantism.

With the hope that their labor would initiate a second Reformation, the writers' main purpose was to reform the Church of England and reunite all churches of the Reformed faith in Britain, in a manner consistent with the Word of God. Episcopalians, Independents, Scottish Presbyterians, Erastians (a group that advocated supremacy of the state over the church), and three commissioners from the Reformed Church of France all participated in the assembly. But the majority of members were English Presbyterians.

What the Westminster Assembly produced was impressive: the Westminster Confession, the Form of Presbyterian Church Government, a Directory of Public Worship, the Larger Catechism (for preaching) and the Shorter Catechism (for instruction of children). But the assembly never achieved its primary goals. Because it was cut off from Parliamentary authority when Oliver Cromwell came to power in 1648, the Westminster Standards were not used to unite Protestants in Britain. Although they ably served to summarize thought about the Protestant Reformation, they did not start a second one. Content to categorize and arrange material in a logical manner, the Westminster Standards were unable to respond to the advent of the new scientific age (the Royal Society was founded while they were in session). Those who used the documents in later centuries often remained on the defensive, both theologically and intellectually.

In a masterful study, John Leith has drawn attention to the strengths and weaknesses of Westminster.[14] The Confession, as he points out, was arranged around four major themes: the Holy Scripture, the lordship and sovereignty of God, the covenant, and the Christian life.[15] The last section comprises over two-thirds of the entire document and had a powerful impact on the development of Presbyterian churches, as well as Baptist and Congregational churches, in Britain and the United States.

Certainly few theological documents can rival the Confession or the two catechisms for the precise biblically-based propositions they contain. Presbyterians may still study the sections about God, the Trinity, and the Sacraments with great benefit. And the catechism answers (which some of us learned by heart as children) provide concise and meaningful responses to difficult questions. Few will ever forget the answer to the first question about the chief end of man (humanity) in the Shorter Catechism: to glorify and enjoy God forever.

Nevertheless, as Leith demonstrates, by writing only with propositional logic, the Westminster divines often ignored the emerging rationality that scientific study was beginning to supply. By concentrating on abstractions and ignoring history, they sacrificed relevance and liveliness; by focusing on matters of truth and skirting tolerance, they produced documents that often appear to be stuffy and inflexible today. By insisting on the literal inspiration of Scripture, Westminster necessitated the writing of subsequent confessions that understood the Bible in light of higher criticism and modern discoveries in archaeology and biblical languages. Restudy of the Westminster documents demonstrates why they served Presbyterians so long and so well. It also shows why we had to move beyond them in 1967 and 1991, and why confessional statements frequently need to be rewritten to express new understandings of the Christian faith.

As Leith puts it, "Those who stand in the Reformed tradition, especially the English-speaking tradition, have been shaped by the Westminster Confession as by no other Christian creed. Even in rebellion against it, men [*sic*] have been formed by it. . . . Only those who have learned to appreciate its excellence as a statement of the Reformed faith can either understand the faith or merit the right to criticize the Confession negatively."[16]

Questions for Study

1. Do you agree with the Westminster Confession when it says all things necessary for life are set down in Scripture and that nothing is ever to be added in the future, whether revelations of the Spirit or human traditions (C-6.006)?

2. *What are the implications for the Christian life when the confession says that "there is no sin so small but it deserves damnation" and "no sin so great that it can bring damnation upon those who truly repent" (C-6.084)?*

The Heidelberg Catechism

Because of his keen interest in Protestant theology and Reformed unity, Frederick III, the Elector of the Palatinate in Germany, encouraged the composition of two theological documents that had profound influence on Reformed churches in Europe, the United States, and all over the world. In 1572 they were adopted by the Church of Scotland (along with the Scots Confession and Calvin's *Catechism*). In 1967 they were included in the *Book of Confessions* with seven other documents as representative of Reformed expressions of faith.

The first of these, the Heidelberg Catechism, was written in 1562 by Zacharias Ursinus and Kaspar Olevianus at the request of Frederick. It is organized around three questions raised in Romans 7:24–25. How great is my sin and wretchedness? How am I freed from my sins? What gratitude do I owe to God for redemption?

The catechism is thus divided into three main sections: Man's Misery, Man's Redemption, and Thankfulness. The second section contains careful expositions of the Trinity, the Apostles' Creed, and the meaning of the Sacraments. The third portion discusses the Ten Commandments, Prayer, and the Lord's Prayer.

The Heidelberg Catechism is also organized into fifty-two units in order to be used each Sunday of the year for teaching sermons. For centuries, Christians in the Reformed tradition have used it to learn about the fundamentals of the Christian faith. Many years ago, some of us who were preparing for the ministry at Hope College attended a Christian Reformed church where the pastor preached on the catechism each Sunday. I still remember the dorm discussions and debates that followed all week, as we cut our theological teeth on this careful statement of faith.

By ending on a note of praise and doxology for God, the Heidelberg Catechism powerfully reminds us how we should close all our prayers and statements of faith: "We ask all this of thee because, as our King, thou art willing and able to give us all that is good since thou hast power over all things, and that by this not we ourselves but thy holy name may be glorified forever" (Question 128).

Today we would probably arrange the catechism in a different order. Following Calvin's faith precepts, we would no doubt start and end with thanksgiving to Christ. For in realizing first how great the forgiveness is that we have in Christ, we are then moved to ask how we have been saved. Only when we appreciate the enormous price Jesus paid for sin can we understand how terrible our sin and the sin of the world is; but this discovery leads again to thanksgiving, because knowing that we are already forgiven, we rejoice that sin no longer controls or dominates us.[17] As the Brief Statement of Faith expresses it in opening and closing statements, "In life and death we belong to God. Through the grace of our Lord Jesus Christ, the love of God, and the communion of the Holy Spirit, we trust in the one triune God" (10:1). "With believers in every time and place, we rejoice that nothing in life or in death can separate us from the love of God in Christ Jesus our Lord" (10.5).

The Second Helvetic Confession

Like many of our confessional statements, the Second Helvetic Confession grew out of struggle and controversy. Originally it was written during 1562–64 by Heinrich Bullinger, a Reformed pastor in Zurich. He intended it as a statement to be included in his will because he did not expect to survive the plague that was decimating his city. When Frederick was being tried in 1566 for heresy, because of his involvement with the publication of the Heidelberg Catechism, he sought Bullinger's help. In response, Bullinger sent his statement of faith, which later became the Second Helvetic Confession.

Centered around thirty major theological theses, the confession begins (as Westminster does) with a description of the centrality of Scripture. It then proceeds to discussions of major issues of faith, concerns about the governance and worship of the church, and about family matters, and concludes with a proper understanding of the relationship between church and state.

Usually the Second Helvetic Confession is understood as primarily pastoral and moderate in tone. Certainly the faith and experience of Bullinger as a Reformed pastor is evident throughout, and as a guide for those engaged in ministry it is still invaluable.[18]

Nevertheless it is not clear that it is entirely irenic. Although Bullinger accepted the declarations of certain previous church councils (5.078) and says cautiously that "we modestly dissent" with those who have different views (5.011), the confession is a product of its time, forged in the violent controversies of the Reformation. Almost every chapter ends with a comment on heresies, sects, or "Questions" (see 5.103, 104, 149, 192, 221, 257 for examples). Furthermore, believers are encouraged to draw the sword against all malefactors and to wage war in the name of God if it will ensure safety (5.255, .256). Perhaps we merely betray our own hopes and dreams when we look for faith statements that are more tolerant than our own, forgetting that even though controversy is painful and can be destructive to unity, it also provides a valuable witness to believers yet to be born about what it means to believe and act in the light of our own time and place.[19]

Questions for Study

1. *Why does the Heidelberg Catechism put so much emphasis on the Ten Commandments and the Lord's Prayer (Questions 92–129)? Are the interpretations there helpful for the church today?*

2. *People still ask Presbyterians what our position is on Free Will and Predestination. What does the Second Helvetic Confession teach us about this difficult subject (C-5.043–.061)?*

The Scots Confession

The Scots Confession of 1560 was written in four days by John Knox, John Douglas, John Row, John Spottiswood, John Willock, and John Winram for the new Scottish Parliament. It reflects far more than ninety-six hours of work; it summarizes six lifetimes of study, prayer, preaching, and courage in the face of danger, conflict, and death. John Knox, for example, had returned just fifteen months before from five years of exile in France. His experiences during the long and trying period before 1560 demonstrate the painful birth of the Church of Scotland: seeing mentors and friends burned at the stake in St. Andrews, serving eighteen months as a French galley slave, and struggling through violent political and spiritual contests with the queens of England and Scotland. Knox had a battle-hardened faith at his fingertips just waiting for expression and dissemination. No wonder his prayer was, "O God, give me Scotland or I die!"

Aside from serving as a primary document that records the confessional origins of the Presbyterian church, the Scots Confession also stands as a textbook of the essential elements of Reformed theology. It deals with all the central affirmations of the Reformed faith (see G-2.0100–.0500): the majesty, holiness, and creative power of God (C-3.01–3.02); the election of God's people for service and salvation (3.08); covenant life marked by a concern for others (3.14; 3.25); and the recognition of the human tendency to idolatry and tyranny (3.03, .16, .18). The basic doctrines are also covered: grace through Jesus Christ alone, faith alone, and scripture alone.

The section on scripture (3.19) has long served to express what Presbyterians believe about the Bible. We confess that we do not look for fancy interpretations but believe in the plain meaning of the Word. When we compare passages in the Bible we look first and last at the absolute centrality of the teachings of Jesus, and we rely on the Holy Spirit—rather than the writings of others or our own understanding—to lead us to truth. Finally, and perhaps most important, the Scots Confession

teaches us that the key to understanding is the "rule of love."
What this means in today's terms is that any interpretation of the
Bible that cannot be sustained by Jesus' command to love God
and love our neighbor as ourselves is a false one; that any judgment we make of other people—whether they are of a different
opinion, a different race, a different nationality, or a different
sexual background—which cannot be sustained by the principle
of love, even if we think it comes from the Bible, is a false judgment.

This principle, which may be shocking to some people who
wish to use the Bible to condemn others, comes directly out of
one of the major principles of the Protestant Reformation: justification by faith alone. When we think of justification by faith
we realize that Martin Luther, John Calvin, and John Knox were
right when they preached that nothing we can do is good enough
to save us from the power of sin. We must depend solely on our
faith and the life, death, and resurrection of our Lord Jesus
Christ.[20]

Sections in the Scots Confession on the definition and governance of the Kirk and the right administration of the sacraments
still provide valuable guidelines for the church's faith and practice.

Considering the dangerous and painful time that the Scottish
reformers endured prior to 1560, their fundamental confidence
in the future and their absolute trust in God is inspiring. Even the
language used throughout the confession demonstrates this
strong assurance:

> we confess and acknowledge (C-3.01, .02, .14, .15, .24)
> we constantly believe (3.04)
> we most surely believe (3.05)
> we acknowledge and confess (3.07)
> so we confess, and most undoubtedly believe (3.08)
> we undoubtedly believe (3.10)
> we do not doubt (3.11)
> we confess and avow (3.24)
> we constantly believe (3.25)

Their fundamental faith and belief that God guides believers through all conflicts and uncertainties is a hopeful message for Presbyterians who have their own hard years ahead.

Questions for Study

1. *How do you think the "rule of love" should be used to interpret Scripture in your congregation today? How should it provide guidance when Presbyterians debate issues of doctrine and ethics?*
2. *The Scots Confession ends as much with a curse as a blessing (C-3.25). How do Christians get rid of anger which is caused by false accusations and violence against them?*

The Apostles' Creed

The Apostles' and Nicene Creeds are the oldest faith documents found in our *Book of Confessions*. The study of the creeds is often called *symbolics* because the Greek word to denote a creed is *symbolon*. A creed differs from a confession or a catechism because it is a short statement of faith that begins with personal words of commitment, "I believe" (*credo* in Latin). A confession is a longer statement of faith for the whole community, whereas a catechism is made up of a series of questions and answers about the essence of the Christian doctrine.

Although the Apostles' Creed traditionally is traced back to the writings of the apostles who followed Jesus, it did not appear in its final form until the ninth century. Parts of it, however, are already found in New Testament confessions (see Mark 8:29; Matt. 28:19; Rom. 1:3–4; 10:9; 1 Cor. 8:6; 12:3; 15:3–7; 2 Cor. 13:13; Phil. 2:6–11; 1 John 4:2–6; 5:5); in statements by the early second-century church leaders Ignatius of Antioch and Justin Martyr; and in creedal summaries like the *Epistula Apostolorum* (around 150 A.D.) and the *Profession of the Presbyters of Smyrna* (around 180).[21]

In its early versions, the Apostles' Creed probably functioned primarily as a statement of faith to be repeated by newly baptized members of the church. In the Presbyterian Church it has often been used as a regular element of worship and for teaching children the essentials of faith in confirmation classes. It also serves as an excellent basis for a sermon series on the fundamentals of faith and can easily be broken down into more than twenty different propositions to be explored.[22]

The version of the Apostles' Creed found in *The Presbyterian Hymnal* is based on a form of the creed finalized in the ninth century, and some question whether all parts of it should be included in worship today. The expression "descended into hell," for example, was added in the fifth century and reflects a second-century belief that entered the New Testament at its latest stages (see 1 Peter 3:18–20) and is very difficult to interpret. It speculates about Jesus descending to preach to tortured spirits in Hades, but it does not appear in the Nicene Creed and some other confessions and catechisms. Considered optional in the *The Hymnbook* (1955),[23] there are good reasons to be hesitant about accepting its inclusion. It is questionable whether Jesus was ever so totally separated from God—even in death—that he could be said to have been in "Hell." What is more, the statement contradicts what is consistently found in the rest of the New Testament, that Jesus was crucified, died, was buried, and was raised on the third day.

Questions for Study

1. *Years ago the Apostles' Creed was read every Sunday in most Presbyterian Churches. Do you think it should be regularly included in our services today?*

2. *Should the words "the Holy Ghost" be changed to "the Holy Spirit" to avoid misconceptions in a culture that often portrays ghosts and angels in television shows and movies in misleading ways?*

The Nicene Creed

The Nicene Creed is the oldest official doctrinal statement of the Christian church and is the best known and most widely used in all branches of Christendom. It grew out of a theological debate in the fourth century about the nature and person of Jesus, when believers wondered if he was equal with God or only like God. In A.D. 325, at the Council of Nicaea called by the emperor Constantine, leaders decided to reject the teaching of Arius that the Son was inferior and subordinate to the Father. Over the next fifty years, the subject continued to dominate Christian study and attention, until the next ecumenical council was held at Constantinople in 381. There, leaders decided to reaffirm the statement of 325 and officially adopt the language that Jesus Christ is "of one essence with the Father." It is this version from 381 A.D. (not the one written in Nicaea) that we use in the church today.

Presbyterians can understand without much difficulty what the debate was all about. We make it clear at the beginning of our *Constitution* that what we believe about Jesus Christ is the heart of who we are and what we decide to do (G-1.0100). We know that the creeds and confessions bear witness to "God's grace in Jesus Christ" (G-2.0100) and that membership and ordination are defined primarily in terms of our commitment to Christ (G-5.0100, 6.0101, 14.0405b(1)). We also need to understand who Jesus is, and what is more, to know how inclusive our church must be (G-5.0103, 9.0102, .0105) and to make sure we use language during worship that allows all members to participate fully and regularly in it (W-1.2006, 1.4003, 3.1003).

As John Leith points out, what the church believes about Jesus' relationship to God is also important in a final sense. It provides the last word about God's plan for humanity and closes the door to speculation that someone else could appear who might represent God more clearly.[24] Since we believe that Jesus is one with God, is God of God, Light of Light, Very God of Very God, begotten not made, there is no more to worry about regarding this kernel of our faith, in this life or the life to come.[25]

Questions for Study

1. What does it mean in an ecological age and in a time of satellite telescopes to say that God is maker of all things "visible and invisible"?

2. *If light is the building block of the universe as we know it, what does it mean to say that Jesus Christ is "Light of Light"?*

The Confession of 2067

Imagine this scenario. The year is 2060. At the meeting of the General Assembly in San Juan (Puerto Rico has been a state for more than fifty years), the new Moderator asks you to serve on the committee that will write the draft of a new confession to be voted on in seven years. What theological, social, cultural, scientific, and political issues will be the most important for your committee to consider?

Such a question is likely to become a reality some day. Since confessions are dated documents and need to reflect the faith, needs, and concerns of contemporary believers, it is safe to assume that a new confession will be produced sometime in the twenty-first century.

At the celebration of the centenary of the Confession of 1967, the committee will have to consider:

- the basic structure of previous confessions
- the essential tenets of the Reformed faith
- current beliefs about the authority of Scripture
- expected concerns the Presbyterian Church will have to deal with between 2067 and the writing of the next confession in the twenty-second century

If each generation needs to have its own confession to reaffirm basic Christian beliefs, as well as to make a statement about the concerns of the current age, what are the issues that will engage your committee? What kind of language will you use? What models of God will be meaningful?

Perhaps some of the following concerns will need to be included:

- continuing dialogue about the authority of the Bible in a church deeply divided about the issue

- a new expression of the meaning of "Christ in us" and a changing appreciation of the role of the Holy Spirit in our lives
- a desire for deeper spirituality in an increasingly stressful world
- a profound commitment to ecumenism and interfaith cooperation in the face of pervasive secularism
- a statement calling for countries to outlaw war as an instrument of national policy
- the expression of concern about the growing gap between the rich and the poor
- statements reflecting continuing struggles with the definition of Christian sexual ethics, both in and out of marriage
- affirmation of the rights of all people regardless of sexual preference or orientation
- continuing concern about our role in the preservation of God's creation; recognition of the uniqueness of the planet earth, while struggling with the concept of the incarnation after the discovery of intelligent life forms in 2042 in the next solar system
- a call for the need for privacy in a world where most communication is through the airwaves and all people are exposed to video, audio, and Web scrutiny
- an abiding concern for the opportunities presented by genetic research

According to the *Book of Order*, "the creeds and confessions of this church reflect a particular stance within the history of God's people" (G-2.0500b). Which of the suggestions made above will actually become a part of our confessional position? What do you think Presbyterians will need to confess and affirm tomorrow or deep into the next century?

Guided by the Confessions

The *Book of Order* tells us that the *Book of Confessions* may be used to

> *guide* the church in its study and interpretation of the
> Scriptures
> *direct* the church in maintaining sound doctrines
> *equip* the church for its work of proclamation (G-
> 2.0100b)

But what purpose is this book to serve in the life of the future church? The debates in the late 1990s about ordination requirements demonstrate in a frightening way that some Presbyterians think it should be used as a moral guidebook or ethical directive to tell us whether certain kinds of behaviors qualify members to be admitted as officers or not. We need to remember, however, that the *Book of Confessions* was not created to provide a unified ethical or theological message or standard, but that it is a library of statements of faith that witnesses to the beliefs of the church catholic and to the development of the Reformed faith. Expressed in different ways and at various times, the confessions outline what the primary Reformed principles are: grace alone, faith alone, scripture alone. The *Book of Confessions* does not exist principally to guide us strictly along ethical paths. It may be used by the church as it was intended, or it may be abused and employed for inappropriate purposes.

We abuse the *Book of Confessions* if we forget that it is a "subordinate standard" in the church, always subject to the authority of Jesus Christ, as the Scriptures bear witness to him, and subordinate to Scripture (G-2.0200). As Shirley Guthrie puts it (following Karl Barth), the confessions are by definition "fragmentary insights" into God's revelation in Jesus Christ and are "given for the moment" by a Christian community in a restricted geographical and chronological setting.[26]

We abuse the *Book of Confessions* if we forget that confessions represent a particular faith statement from a specific moment in history and can be amended from time to time. As Presbyterians we have proclaimed ourselves to be open to the creative work of the Holy Spirit, as Reformed and always ready to be reformed by God (G-2.0200). The confessions provide standards of faith and doctrine, but they are not the primary or only standards.

It can also be abused if we go in another direction and think, as some may now think, that because the confessions can potentially be used incorrectly, they are worthless and should be ignored altogether. Barth reminds us that even if the confessions do not have the authority of scripture they still have "a non-binding authority which must be taken seriously."[27] Confessions may have "relative authority," but the authority is still real. And since all who are ordained vow to be instructed by them as they lead the people of God (G-14.0207c; see the discussion of ordination vows in chapter 7 below), we need to remember that our Presbyterian and Reformed heritage is not one we want to cast lightly aside. Confessional standards about the nature of God, the Bible, the sacraments, and the definition and purpose of the church are not cavalierly drawn up or intended to be easily dismissed.

As we seek to understand what the confessions can do and cannot do, we need not focus on the negative. Barth's comment about dogmatics helps us value their use even if they do not answer all our questions definitively. "With quiet sobriety and sober quietness, we shall do our work in this way. We must use our knowledge as it has been given to us to-day. No more can be required of us than is given to us. And like a servant who is faithful in little, we must not be sorrowful about such little. More than this faithfulness is not required of us."[28]

The *Book of Confessions* provides us with a theological perspective of where we have been and where we are going; it signals to us who we are and who we are to become. It reminds us what it means to be Reformed and always in the process of being reformed by God. If we cut ourselves off from our roots, we will no longer be Presbyterians and we will no longer have a witness that brings a historic message to the future church.

Chapter 7

The Ordination Vows

The First Vow:
The Foundation of Ministry

*T*he purpose of the first ordination question for church officers and pastors seems obvious: "Do you trust in Jesus Christ your Savior?" (see G-14.0405b(1)). Who would want to be a leader in the Presbyterian Church without believing in Jesus Christ? Yet it is essential to begin such an important moment at the heart of faith. There are many goals, purposes, and hidden agendas in ministry, and our attention may easily be deflected from the centrality of our mission, which is to follow Jesus Christ as his disciples (Mark 1:18; 10:28). As James Stewart says in his seminal book on preaching, "Why are we in this work at all? To bring . . . [people] to God through Jesus Christ. That is the ultimate goal of all our striving, the purpose of our commission. It ought to be our one consuming ambition to help men and women . . . to meet the living God."[1]

Indeed, the first principle of leadership is the same one required to become a member. "One becomes an active member of the church through faith in Jesus Christ as Savior and acceptance of his Lordship in all of life" (G-5.0101a). When new members profess their faith they are immediately asked who their Lord and Savior is, whether they trust in him, and whether or not they intend to be his disciples, obey his word, and show his love.

For Presbyterians the answers to these questions should not be taken for granted. Paul reminds us in 1 Corinthians 3:11 that faith in Jesus Christ is the foundation of the ministry of the church, and that "a skilled master builder" (literally, "a wise architect" in Greek, v. 10) will always start there. Foundations are important in buildings and in ministry and it is important to know what rock bottom is.

But what does it mean to have Jesus Christ as the foundation of faith and ministry? For church officers and pastors today it is essential to recommit ourselves to the premise that even though we often fail God through our own sinfulness, pride, and lack of self-confidence, we are still determined to make Jesus Christ and his will the center of our ministries and private lives. That way, when life gets off balance, when the world becomes full of alteration and unpredictability, or when we change our minds about theology, politics, or ethics, we know that we continue to have a center that serves as home base. We know that Jesus Christ is still the most important person, the most important role model, the most important thought in life and ministry.

For us this kind of faith can be complex and simple all at once. When we come up against hard times, when we have tough decisions to make for ourselves or for the church, we have three resources: return to Jesus Christ as center, study the Scriptures in prayer, and try to imagine what Christ would do in the same situation or what he would have us do in a situation he never had to face. Even though many argue today that little can be known about the Jesus of history, people of faith know that his will is always available to those who trust in him and seek his presence.

Jesus Christ is the primary standard of the Christian life, and it is important for us to know which standards can be altered and which ones need to remain the same. As we read in 2 Timothy 1:13–14, "Hold to the standard of sound teaching that you have heard from me, in the faith and love that are in Christ Jesus. Guard the good treasure entrusted to you, with the help of the Holy Spirit living in us."

As church officers, there is nothing more important than our commitment to Jesus Christ. Jesus should be the center of all of our preaching, all our teaching, all our decision making, indeed, of everything we do and say: "whatever you do, in word or deed, do everything in the name of the Lord Jesus, giving thanks to God . . . through him" (Col. 3:17). Presbyterians do not need special mottos to proclaim who they are. Every congregation should be a church where Jesus Christ is always at the center.

Questions for Study

1. *How do you know what Christ wants you to do and be as one of his disciples?*
2. *If Christ is always kept as the center of your congregation, can you think of ways that things might change in your church?*

Do You Accept the Scriptures?

The Scriptures of the Old and New Testaments are the absolute guide for faith and action for the Presbyterian Church (U.S.A.). There is no other standard which provides a better or more powerful norm. Whenever Presbyterians discuss or debate a matter of belief or a controversial issue of Christian ethics, they always turn to the Bible to determine positions, process, and direction. As the Confession of 1967 puts it, "The Scriptures are not a witness among others, but the witness without parallel" (C-9.27).

It is with a certain amount of sadness, nevertheless, that we consider the second question asked of all pastors, elders, and deacons before ordination or installation: "Do you accept the Scriptures of the Old and New Testaments to be, by the Holy Spirit, the unique and authoritative witness to Jesus Christ in the Church universal, and God's Word to you?" (G-14.0405b).[2]

The problem for Presbyterians is that not every officer or member means the same thing by that vow. As a study received by the 194th General Assembly of the United Presbyterian

Church indicates, there are at least five different positions within our denomination regarding the proper interpretation of the Scriptures.[3] These perspectives range on a wide continuum from the literal interpretation of the Bible (the Bible is without error in all matters) to the view that "the Bible is merely a record of the moral and religious experiences of Hebrews and Christians." According to a survey conducted at the time, 48 percent of Presbyterians took a position consistent with the Confession of 1967, agreeing that "All of the Bible is both the inspired Word of God and at the same time a thoroughly human document." As the Confession of 1967 says, "The Bible is to be interpreted in the light of its witness to God's work of reconciliation in Christ. The Scriptures, given under the guidance of the Holy Spirit, are nevertheless the words of men [sic], conditioned by the language, thought forms, and literary fashions of the places and times at which they were written. They reflect views of life, history, and the cosmos which were then current. The church, therefore, has an obligation to approach the Scriptures with literary and historical understanding" (C-9.29).

Such a distribution of opinions inevitably leads to controversy, and it is fair to say that nearly every major issue that Presbyterians have debated within the past thirty years has returned, in one way or the other, to the critical debate about the authority of the Bible.[4]

Important questions for our life and work together are at issue. What is the Bible? Is it a book or a library? What do we do when we find differing perspectives on the Scriptures? Do we believe in a particular theory about the composition of the Bible or do we believe in the God and the Lord Jesus Christ who are revealed there? How do we treat other Presbyterians when we radically disagree, not only about the interpretation of a particular passage but about the definition of the Bible as a whole?

The most difficult question we need to ask ourselves as a denomination is severe—namely, is it possible for Presbyterians to remain one church when we cannot agree about the way the Bible is to be used and interpreted, or is it time for conservatives and liberals to go their own ways? Is it time to write each other off either as unbelievers or hopelessly misguided interpreters, or are there still reasons to continue the struggle, hoping that in spite of frustration and pain we can still learn about God from each other because we are members of one family of faith?

In my own view, although years of careful Bible study and preaching have convinced me of the basic correctness of the position of the Confession of 1967, I do not want to end the dialogue and discussion with those who think otherwise. The second ordination question points us in the right direction when it urges us to use Scripture in conjunction with the present activity of the Holy Spirit in our lives. A statement adopted by the 123rd General Assembly of the Presbyterian Church in the United States (1983) remains valuable. "This guideline for interpretation is not just a pious platitude. Neither careful rationale nor logical deduction, nor use of all the tools of critical-historical exegesis, can guarantee the right interpretation of Scripture. After we have done the best we can with all the means at our disposal, we depend on God's Spirit to enable us rightly to hear and believe and obey."[5] It is through prayer and dialogue with others that we can best discover what the Spirit is saying to us through the Bible today.

The ordination question that church officers affirm, furthermore, asks them to use the Bible, not to find some unalterable theological or ethical position, but to find Jesus Christ, who is the Word of God in human flesh, and to seek for God's will through him. Again, the statement of the Presbyterian Church in the United States is helpful. "At the most direct level of application, this principle means that any teaching of the Bible on a matter of faith or life is to be used in a manner consistent with scriptural accounts of Jesus' own teaching and embodiment of the person and will of God."[6] In other words, even though recent studies of the historical Jesus indicate how difficult it is to know precisely what Jesus did or said, we are still obligated as Presbyterians to try to discover what Jesus, the living Word, wills for us and to make his will the priority in all our study of the Bible.

If we see a conflict, for example, between certain Old Testament precepts and the teaching of Jesus, we should have little trouble choosing between the two. To paraphrase something P. T. Forsyth once wrote: Biblical preaching preaches Christ and uses the Bible; it does not preach the Bible and use Christ.[7]

The Bible will not allow us to come as slaves who take it simply as command or at face value. Who is commanding and whose values are we using to face it? What do modern studies of the Scriptures have to teach us? What do recent examinations of Greek and Hebrew literature show us about the proper interpretation? With all the archaeological discoveries that occur almost every month in Israel, Jordan, Turkey, Italy, and Greece, what wonderful new insights are about to be exposed to light? The Bible is not a simple book waiting for simple minds to grasp it. One does not have to check one's intellect in a coatroom when he or she walks into a church each Sunday. God gave us brains with which to think and ask questions. Naive belief has never been a priority for Presbyterians, but, rather, knowledgeable conviction, informed by the newest discoveries and grounded in the tradition of the faith.

Perhaps one way to look at the constant struggle that intelligent people of faith have had to endure is in terms of "freedom in harness."[8] Freedom because the Holy Spirit directs us to find new truth every day. Freedom because we can easily see the great liberty with which the first evangelists wrote—when Matthew and Luke revised Mark's words of Jesus, and John ventured off on his own. Freedom because the same Spirit who inspired the writers of the Scriptures also inspires the preachers and hearers of today and the future. Freedom because believers of every age and culture must reunderstand and reinterpret the Scriptures to make them their own.

Yet we are also "in harness" at the same time. "Tamed by the Holy Spirit" (which is a good translation for the word *meek* in Matt. 5:5),[9] moving easy in harness; yoked by the master (Matt. 11:29–30) for efficient ministry; harnessed to Reformed tradition about the plain text of Scripture and the rule of love (Scots

Confession, C-3.18), but still very much free in Christ (2 Cor. 3:17; Gal. 5:1, 13).

Calvin expresses the struggle of using and understanding the Bible, and his words serve as an excellent reminder about the nature of faith: "If we turn aside from the Word. . . , though we may strive with strenuous haste, yet, since we have got off the track, we shall never reach the goal. For we should so reason that the divine countenance, which even the apostle calls 'unapproachable' [1 Tim. 6:16], is for us like an inexplicable labyrinth unless we are conducted into it by the thread of the Word; so that it is better to limp along this path than to dash with all speed outside it."[10]

No doubt, Presbyterians will continue to debate the proper interpretation of the second ordination question for years to come. Let it be hoped that we will choose to continue that dialogue, as difficult as it may be, understanding that it has always been in that crucible that Presbyterians have pounded out what it means to hear God's Word afresh and—within the struggle that each new generation has—discovered what it means to have God call them through Christ to act and believe. As the Confession of 1967 affirms, "In each time and place, there are particular problems and crises through which God calls the church to act. The church, guided by the Spirit, humbled by its own complicity and instructed by all attainable knowledge, seeks to discern the will of God and learn how to obey in these concrete situations" (C-9.43).

Questions for Study

1. *Can you think of ways the interpretation of the Bible has been a major influence in the life of the Presbyterian church? Think, for example, of the Civil War, the debate about evolution, the struggle for integration, and the women's movement.*

2. *What issues in the future will put our understanding of Scripture to the test?*

Question Three: Essential Tenets
of the Reformed Tradition

The one vow that may be the most difficult for lay people to understand is found in the third question, "Do you sincerely receive and adopt the *essential tenets of the Reformed faith* as expressed in the confessions of our Church as authentic and reliable expositions of what Scripture leads us to believe and do, and will you be instructed and led by those confessions as you lead the people of God?"

For those not trained in theology and church history, these solemn words raise a question about what it really means to be part of the Reformed tradition. How do Presbyterians at the beginning of the twenty-first century affirm the belief of the Reformers of the sixteenth century that the church must be reformed, not according to human tradition but by the Word of God found in the Old and New Testaments? Short of taking a course at a college or theological seminary or studying the *Book of Confessions* in detail, is there a nutshell definition of our heritage that can point the new officer in the right direction? Fortunately, despite the complexity of Reformed history, the *Book of Order* provides adequate beginning definitions.

The place to start, of course, is with *Jesus Christ*. Just as the first ordination question asks whether officers trust in Jesus Christ as Lord and Savior, so the first words of the *Book of Order* point to him as the beginning and end of faith. "All power in heaven and earth is given to Jesus Christ" (G-1.0100).

Another major principle of the Reformed faith is the first of the "Historic Principles of Church Order," which points to the concept of *Christian freedom*, that all believers are responsible, foremost, to God in their faith and actions, since "God alone is Lord of the conscience, and hath left it free from the doctrines and commandments" of human beings (G-1.0301). This principle, as is often pointed out, involves the concept of "the sovereignty of God," that is, the majesty, holiness, and providence of

God who rules the world in righteousness and love (see G-2.0500a).

Another key concept of the Presbyterian interpretation of the Reformed faith has to do with the knowledge that our church is not static but is always open to the Holy Spirit and the change which the Spirit's fresh breeze inevitably brings. According to the *Book of Order*, the church, in obedience to Jesus Christ, is always ready to reform doctrine and polity. "The church affirms 'Ecclesia reformata, semper reformanda,' that is, 'The church reformed, always reforming,' according to the Word of God and the call of the Spirit" (G-2.0200; also see 18.0101). Central to this belief is the acknowledgment that the session of every church is charged with leading "the congregation continually to discover what God is doing in the world and to plan for change, renewal, and reformation under the Word of God" (G-10.0102j).

In a valuable study of the expression "the church reformed, always reforming," Michael D. Bush urges Presbyterians to be careful how they understand and use it.[11] The concept of change, he contends, is not one that makes the world different because progress is needed, or alters things because life is stifling if it stays the same. The change that is meant in the Reformed tradition is always consistent with God's Word and takes place because God wills it. In his opinion, the translation "the church reformed, always reforming" is incorrect and misleading and should be rendered "the church reformed must always be reformed," that is, according to the Word and by God, not by us. His translation affirms what we already know: that the Reformation continues because human beings continue to make mistakes; that it is always a matter of God's grace and nothing we plan or do (reformation is God's work, not ours); and the idea of a church that is Reformed and perpetually reforming indicates that we are part of an institution that is always willing to repent. The call to reform is not exclusively to be relevant or innovative: it is to be faithful to the God who has the power to make all things new.

The Presbyterian Church (U.S.A.), furthermore, identifies

with other key affirmations of the Protestant Reformation whose focus is in the rediscovery of God's grace in Jesus Christ and what are called "the Protestant watchwords": grace alone, faith alone, and Scripture alone (G-2.0400). It is by the reaffirmation of these principles, chiefly as expressed by Paul in Romans 1:16–17; 3:27–28; and Galatians 2:15–21, that the church recenters itself in faith in Jesus Christ and not in what we do to impress God with our works and actions.

In the *Book of Confessions* the Presbyterian Church (U.S.A.) expresses the faith of the Reformed tradition in detail. Some of the great themes of this faith are summarized briefly in G-2.0500 as:

> The *election* of the people of God for service as well as salvation;
>
> *Covenant life* marked by a disciplined concern for order in the church *according to the Word of God*;
>
> A *faithful stewardship* that shuns ostentation and seeks the proper use of the gifts of God's creation;
>
> The *recognition of the human tendency to idolatry* and tyranny, which calls the people of God to work for the transformation of society by seeking justice and living in obedience to the Word of God.

As Reformed Christians, we also believe it is not just the Presbyterian Church that is being called by God to be open to redirection by the Word of God and the Holy Spirit, but that all denominations stand under that same authority, as the whole church is called "to a new openness to God's continuing reformation of the Church ecumenical, that it might be a more effective instrument of mission in the world" (G-3.0401d). Such an understanding recognizes that Presbyterians are required by God to participate in ecumenical ministries and see themselves as one part of the church universal.

In addition to these "tenets" of the Reformed tradition,[12] new officers will also want to turn to the Directory for Worship and the *Book of Confessions* to discover the definitions there of the

Protestant belief in the primacy of Scripture and our understanding of the meaning of worship and sacraments.

Clearly, the third ordination question will be a critical one as
our church is tested in the years to come and tries to find ways
to retain its historic beliefs while remaining open at the same
time to the reform and change that God brings us through the
action of the Spirit in the new world in which we will live. Perhaps part of the statement of the 205th General Assembly (1993)
can provide a guideline and a prayer as we try to learn what it
means to be "reformed and always being reformed":

> We are the Church.
> > Yet who are we?
> > > Presbyterian, Reformed
> > > Old New
> > > Tradition Change
> > > Spirit-led Spirit-filled
> We are the Church.
> > And our center, the core of our being
> > > is to worship
> Love
> > Enjoy
> > God forever;
> To worship the gift of God in Christ
> > Emmanuel, God with us.[13]

Questions for Study

1. *Can you think of ways in which our denomination still
   needs reformation?*
2. *Which of the tenets of the Reformed tradition do you think
   is the most important for the future of our denomination?*

The Fourth and Fifth Questions:
In Obedience to Jesus Christ

Will you fulfill your office in obedience to Jesus Christ, under
the authority of Scripture, and be continually guided by our
confessions?

Will you be governed by our church's polity, and will you abide by its discipline? Will you be a friend among your colleagues in ministry, working with them, subject to the ordering of God's Word and Spirit? (G-14.0207d,e)

The fourth ordination question is a reiteration of the first three, focusing again on

- the authority of Jesus Christ in ministry and in life (see the discussion on the first question above)
- the centrality of Scripture
- the essential tenets of the Reformed faith

This question not only asks if new officers *trust, accept, receive,* and *adopt* these statements as *individuals,* but whether or not they will follow them to *fulfill* a *public office* and be held accountable to them in the exercise of their duties.

The fifth question addresses constitutional order and personal relationships, making it clear that elders, deacons, and pastors are obligated to uphold the Form of Government and are not free to obey parts of it and ignore others. Since our church government is representative and has built-in checks and balances, new officers need to be reminded that the vow they take to abide by its discipline is not a static one but may be changed and reformed by the action of the Holy Spirit through an orderly amendment process (G-18.0000–.0302).

The final section of the fifth question asks church officers if they will promise to get along with other Presbyterians. Those with experience in church politics will never question the wisdom of such a vow. All one has to do is attend a few session meetings or sit through the debates in higher governing bodies to realize that the church is a very human institution where people aggravate each other, become angry, and get their feelings hurt.

Paul admonishes Christians not to bite and devour one another, lest they consume one another (Gal. 5:15). The positive side of that warning is expressed in Ephesians 4:3–4, where believers are called to cooperate, build their ministry on love and mutual understanding, and work collegially with others as the Holy Spirit directs. We are urged by our constitution to perform our duties according to the "law of love" (G-6.0304). When Presbyterians cannot get along with each other, it might be worth a moment during services of worship to remember the vow we have all taken, a promise that we will all work at being "friends" in ministry.

Questions for Study

1. *How does your calling as a church officer influence your public life? Do you know people who are not good representatives of the church because of the way they act or fail to act?*

2. *What can you do in your own church to enact "the law of love"?*

In Your Own Life

When my wife, Barbara, was ordained as a deacon a few years ago, she cried when she came to the sixth ordination vow. The question, "Will you in your own life seek to follow the Lord Jesus Christ, love your neighbors, and work for the reconciliation of the world?" (G-14.0207f) was so personal and powerful that it overwhelmed her.

Indeed, at some point the vows we take as church officers need to move past the public to the personal. Every officer should have private reasons why she or he wants to become a deacon or elder, and feel from the inside out that God is issuing a call to ministry because there are specific tasks for each individual to do.

The call demands that one's personal life be a model for public office. One who can manage little things is worthy of more responsibility (Luke 16:10). The New Testament sets high standards for church officers and indicates that following Jesus Christ involves shunning passions, pursuing righteousness, faith, love, and peace, and calling on God with a pure heart. It requires the ability to stay out of useless controversies and urges leaders to approach opponents with patience and gentleness (2 Tim. 2:22–25). Bishops and deacons must be above reproach, be temperate, sensible, hospitable, and good managers of their own households. They must be serious, honest, and financially responsible, and hold fast to the mystery of the faith (1 Tim. 3:1–10; compare 6:11–16). These demanding requirements should be enough to make any new officer catch his or her breath.

By promising to love their neighbors, church officers are moved back from the personal to the public sphere. Loving your neighbor means more than loving *our* neighbors; it involves loving *God's* neighbors. Jesus made clear in the parable of the Good Samaritan that my neighbor is not just the person who lives close to me or is nice to me; it is anyone I find in need, anywhere in the journey of life (Luke 10:29–37). By taking a public vow to love my neighbor, I move beyond boundaries of my own yard or apartment and promise that what I do in private will now be something I will enable my congregation to accomplish as a matter of public policy.

When officers finish this vow with a commitment to reconciliation in the whole world, they are taken out of any localized arena in which they live and are now placed in the cosmos that God sent his Son to save (the Greek for "world" is *kosmos*). As the Confession of 1967 makes clear, in doing this we are following our Lord Jesus Christ, who became a man so that human beings could be reconciled to God and to one another (2 Cor. 5:18–20). We are acknowledging our responsibility as church members to work for reconciliation in society, among different religious groups, among nations, between the rich and poor, and in our interpersonal relationships (C-9.41–47).

All of this is a great deal of responsibility for church officers who know that they must serve God with modesty. But the ordination vows do not ask us what we can accomplish *alone*, but what we can achieve with God helping and empowering us. God is not restricted by our personal and public power when it comes to what can be done through us.

Questions for Study

1. *Which of the ordination vows moves you the most person-*
   ally?
2. *How does your congregation define your neighborhood?*

Peace, Unity, and Purity

It is hard to imagine why any Presbyterian officer would not want "to promise to further the peace, unity, and purity of the Church." Yet members of churches and presbyteries all over the country can provide stories of governing bodies in constant turmoil and trouble.

How can that be if every pastor, elder, and deacon has taken the seventh ordination vow? There are always reasons. Legitimate causes of truth must be pursued, differences of opinion debated, various interpretations of the Bible expressed, violations of the *Constitution* examined, hurt feelings healed, and meanness of spirit overcome. Ever since the birth of the Presbyterian Church we have been in conflict over the issues of slavery, evolution, Old School vs. New School, the understanding of the Bible as the infallible Word vs. the principles of higher criticism, the question of ordination, etc.[14]

But why is it so difficult to keep the seventh vow? It cannot be because we lack knowledge of peacemaking. After all these years of having peacemaking as a primary Presbyterian goal, after all the biblical and theological studies we have written and published, we cannot claim ignorance as a cause.

It cannot be a failure to know what unity is. We understand how to achieve oneness of Spirit, as the joining of the northern and southern streams of our church demonstrates, and that is why we call ourselves the Presbyterian Church (U.S.A.).

Is it a lack of purity or a misunderstanding of what purity

means? In the seventh ordination vow, if we consider the historic roots of the promise, it is necessary to understand that what is promised has nothing to do with moral or ethical uprightness. Instead, the word "purity" refers to doctrinal correctness as expressed in the Scriptures and in the confessions of the church. As the Westminster Confession puts it, "this . . . catholic [or universal] Church hath been sometimes more, sometimes less, visible. And particular churches, which are members thereof, are more or less pure, according as the doctrine of the gospel is taught and embraced, ordinances administered, and public worship performed more or less purely in them" (C-6.143). Thus, promising to keep the purity of the church involves what the Scots Confession refers to as preserving "the notes of the true Kirk": the true preaching of the Word of God, the right administration of the sacraments, and ecclesiastical discipline rightly administered (C-3.18).[15] Being ethical and obeying biblical standards of morality is a requirement of being a church officer, but it is not what this vow concerns. It has to do with the way God intends the church to be and the unity it can achieve.

Do we lack the ability or the will to obey God's Word and achieve the unity we say we desire? If we do not have the ability, then we need to admit that sin has control over us and we do not have the power to do what God commands. If we lack the will, then we must confess that other matters of doctrine, biblical interpretation, and social policy are more important than doing what we have promised.

A final reason for our lack of ability or desire is that we are just too self-absorbed as Presbyterians, we are too wrapped up in ourselves as individuals or as congregations and higher governing bodies. If the most important thing Presbyterians can do is achieve internal harmony, all our energy will be expended working on our relationships, rather than developing goals that force us to focus on the ministry of Christ to others. Pursuing peace (Rom. 14:19; 1 Peter 3:11) must mean far more than getting along with each other. Being the Church requires telling

God's truth and striving for justice in the world that Christ came to save (W-7.4000).

Peace, unity, and purity are derived, not from the constant adolescent need to define the identity of members of the community or to determine who is right or who is wrong, but as Ephesians 4 tells us, from spiritual maturity that centers on the call of Christ, "the unity of the Spirit in the bond of peace" (v. 3). Perhaps what the Presbyterian Church needs is not more relationship-building exercises or task forces on reconciliation, but a sincere desire and prayer to grow up into mature Christian adulthood and to get on with the work that Christ has called us to do, without constantly thinking about ourselves.

Questions for Study

1. *How much energy is used up in your church to put out emotional and psychological fires, energy that could be better employed to do the work of the kingdom?*
2. *What do you think the marks of a mature Christian are?*

Energy, Intelligence, and Imagination

The wording of the last ordination question, "Will you seek to serve the people with energy, intelligence, imagination, and love?" is reminiscent of the essential teaching of Jesus in Matthew 22:37: "You shall love the Lord your God with all your heart, and with all your soul, and with all your mind," where believers are called to give their entire selves to God.

That intelligence and imagination should be linked together is verified by the research over the past few years regarding the left and right brain. The ability to reason coupled with the power of human creativity defines our uniqueness. These characteristics are functions of being fashioned in the image of God and make us more like the Creator than other creatures.

This critical relationship is also recognized by ancient biblical writers and is especially evident in a passage like Exodus

31:3–5, where God tells Moses that he has called Bezalel son of Uri to assist in the creation of the Tent of Meeting, the Ark of the Covenant, and the mercy seat: "I have filled him with divine spirit, with ability, intelligence, and knowledge in every kind of craft, to devise artistic designs, to work in gold, silver, and bronze, in cutting stones for setting, and in carving wood, in every kind of craft."

Intelligence has always been important in Presbyterian leadership. Just as Presbyterians were proud that their pastors were among the best educated citizens in colonial days, so at the beginning of the twenty-first century we are still called to prize the fact that our church is governed by those who know how to reason, plan, and learn. Theology is important to us, and we have a responsibility to use the brains God has given us to approach the Scriptures with literary and historical knowledge (C-9.29), to express what we believe in the light of contemporary culture (W-3.1003), and to organize our service to the world using all the assistance that modern technology offers.

Imagination is also critical to the work of Presbyterian officers. It is important in our study of the Scriptures as we enter imaginatively into the world and events portrayed in the Bible to participate in what God does and promises there (W-5.3002c(5)). Imagination helps us express our faith in Christ in fresh ways to one another and to the world.

But of all the promises Presbyterians make when they become officers, the one about serving the people with imagination may ultimately be the most difficult to keep because it seems to run contrary to tradition and a natural inclination to resist change. Presbyterians often say they want innovation, but when it comes to implementation they choose worship, structures, and procedures that are known and comfortable.

As Christians, it is important for us to remember that the exercise of imagination is chiefly a response to the activity of the Holy Spirit in our lives and churches. We see it particularly in the centering of our fellowship in worship. The Reformed concept of worship calls us to use language that is "more expressive than rationalistic" and that "creates ardor as well as order" (W-1.2005). We can worship the Holy God through symbols (using different biblical names for God) and through symbolic actions (fasting and feasting, rejoicing and resting, marching and resting, dancing and clapping hands, making music and singing to the Lord; W-1.2003).

What is more, we may worship our Lord through sound and motion, through the richness of color, texture, and form, and through the creative dimensions of architecture, furnishings, vestments, drama, and language. When these artistic expressions awaken us to God's presence they are appropriate for worship and expand our consciousness of the reality and grace of God (W-1.3034). As the Directory for Worship puts it, "In ordering worship the Church is to seek openness to the creativity of the Holy Spirit, who guides the Church toward worship which is orderly yet spontaneous, consistent with God's Word and open to the newness of God's future" (W-3.1002a).

Carol Doran and Thomas Troeger capture the importance of imagination in a section of their book titled "Opening the Imagination to the Spirit."[16] "We need . . . to be preparing for the Spirit so that our worship can soar like the wind. . . . Our prayer must be open to every form of call and response that passes between God and us." As they put it elsewhere: "Reforming our worship is a way of participating in God's transforming process. It is an act of faithfulness to God who keeps stirring and prodding us to be more completely the people we are meant to be." What they write applies not just to worship, but to all the creative aspects of our work and service as Presbyterian officers.

Questions for Study

1. Can you think of ways that creative imagination could enrich the life of your congregation or of our denomination?

2. How can we keep our promise to direct our "energy" into the life of the church?

Promising Love

Love is the final word when it comes to promises that elders, deacons, and pastors make before God and the church: "Will you seek to serve the people with energy, intelligence, imagination, and *love*?" (G-14.0207h). As Paul reminds us so forcefully in 1 Corinthians 13, without love we are nothing.

Love, of course, is a primary ingredient of all service and all Christian life. As Presbyterians we are charged by God to "care for all that lives" (G-3.0101), "to care for one another in daily living" (W-6.3002), and to demonstrate "the new reality in Christ" by our love for one another (G-3.0300c(2)). In the life of the church, the transforming power of the Holy Spirit is manifest in mutual love and service, in self-giving, and in the exercise of compassion toward the world (W-7.2002, .3003). "Those duties which all Christians are bound to perform by the law of love are especially incumbent upon elders because of their calling to office and are to be fulfilled by them as official responsibilities" (G-6.0304), and deacons are to be known for their brotherly and sisterly love and their warm sympathies (G-6.0401).

When Jesus sought to warn his disciples about the worst catastrophe that could overwhelm the fledgling church, he did not end his discussion with projections of war or rumors of wars; he did not see floods, famines, or earthquakes as the final consequences of sin. Instead, he imagined a horrible scenario in which love is totally absent: "And because of the increase of lawlessness, the love of many will grow cold" (Matt. 24:12; see Rev. 2:4).

Such a disaster could display itself in practical terms when Christians do not love anymore and charity is frozen out, so that

- no pastoral care is provided in times of stress and emergency
- no elders, deacons, or Stephen Ministers are providing a caring ministry
- no one in church forgives a brother or sister for a wrong

- no members cluster together to help one another
- no one loves neighbor as oneself because even self-love is freeze-dried
- no session provides money or prayer support for the mission work of the church
- no evidence can be seen of that which marks the Christian church most distinctively, the hope that comes from love (Rom. 5:5)

Paul reminds us that love is a most important gift of the Holy Spirit (1 Corinthians 13); it is much more than an expression of goodwill or high self-esteem. It comes from God and is God (1 John 4:7–21).

Love, furthermore, is the only characteristic that Paul lists as both a gift and a fruit of the Holy Spirit. Love is the first of the products of the Spirit (Gal. 5:22–23). It is not merely one of the "greater gifts"; it is, as 1 Corinthians 13:13 indicates, the "greatest" of them all, the last and best good that God gives us. It is the love found primarily in the life, passion, death, and resurrection of Jesus Christ.

How love functions in our lives always remains something of a mystery, because it must be freely given. It can never be demanded or required. Love is always a surprise because it has to be released to be acquired.

As Archibald MacLeish put it in one of his poems, love is a mystery which is alive.

> Love is a bird in a fist:
> To hold it hides it, to look at it lets it go. . . .
> There is no answer other to this mystery.[17]

Questions for Study

1. *We talk about love all the time in the church. But what does it mean in practical terms? Whom do we love and what does this love cost?*

2. *Sometimes the kind of love God has for us is called "unbounded generosity." Can you think of examples of how love like that can strengthen the Presbyterian Church?*

Try

One of the most encouraging words in our *Constitution* is "try." An (unofficial) computer search of the *Book of Order* indicates it is found in just one context, and it only appears in four places where it is used at the installation and/or ordination of elders, deacons, ministers, and lay preachers: "in your ministry will you *try* to show the love and justice of Jesus Christ?" (G-14.0207i, .0207j, .0405b(9), .0801e(9); but see D-1.0103 in reference to mediation).

Normally, we emphasize the promise to demonstrate our Lord's love and justice in our lives and ministry. But the trying is also significant because it introduces a level of reality and humility into the vows we make. Many Presbyterians have memories of parents and teachers saying, "I do not want you to *try* to be good. I want you to *be* good!" Here, however, the church actually sanctions, or at least recognizes, the value of an attempt, even if it is unsuccessful.

Any officer of the church can be determined to try to show the compassion and mercy of Jesus Christ. But the attempt may be limited by circumstances, by one's own abilities, by the responses received from those one wants to reach, by the power of enemies, or by the difficulty of discovering God's will in a given situation. As Joan S. Gray and Joyce C. Tucker say in another context, "The candidate for church office may feel like the person in the Gospel account who responded to Jesus, 'I believe, help my unbelief' (Mark 9:24). Doubts about one's abilities and feelings of inadequacy for the task may well be very appropriate early responses to the call to office in the church."[18]

Though it is difficult to know what the authors of this vow originally intended, it is likely that it goes beyond an officer's humility in the face of new responsibilities. Sometimes Christians do not even try to keep their promises. They let apathy, cowardice, or sin prevent them from attempting to love others and fight for justice. At times the inordinate value placed on harmony at any price, concern about keeping friends or retaining a job, a lack of effort to ascertain the facts or a failure to discern the will of God—all prevent us from doing what we say we intend. It is at this point, when our worst impulses rule, that we may thank God that we as leaders are forgiven, not just for our inabilities, but even for our lackadaisical attempts or deliberate refusals to follow our Lord. It reminds us that the final hallmark of a church officer is not success or perfectionism but faithfulness and love.

Questions for Study

1. *Sometimes it is worse to have failed to try than to have merely failed. How is this truth usually accepted by Americans who always want to be number one?*

2. *On occasion, the church really does not try to speak in the name of the gospel or try to work for justice, because it seems politically unrealistic or because members are afraid of the consequences. Can you think of examples where the church has not tried for the kingdom and others have paid the price?*

Chapter 8

Ethical and Professional Standards for Church Officers

General Concepts

*D*uring the past few years it has been necessary for the General Assembly, synods, and presbyteries to develop careful policy manuals in order to provide standards and procedures to deal firmly and fairly with charges of sexual misconduct against pastors, church officers, and other leaders in the church.

Since we live in an era, however, where many problems are solved exclusively in religious or secular courts of law, more general questions need to be raised about the overall responsibilities and rights of church officers and pastors. How do we define the ethical and professional obligations of people who serve the church, and how do we know when they have violated the guidelines that direct their conduct?

According to the Rules of Discipline (D-2.0203), "An offense is any act or omission by a member or an officer of the church that is contrary to the Scriptures or the *Constitution of the Presbyterian Church (U.S.A.)*."

Although this definition may seem rather vague at first glance, closer examination reveals that it has serious and definable guidelines. In order to discover if a church officer is open to charges of misconduct it is necessary to know what the Bible and the *Constitution* require of its leaders.

These guidelines are not new. Prior to reunion, the definition of an offense in the United Presbyterian Church was similar. "An offense is anything in the doctrine, principles, or practice of a church member, officer, or judicatory, which is contrary to the Word of God or to those expositions of its teachings as to faith and practice which are contained in the Constitution" (1960, D-I, 8; wording changed 1983). Similar examples can no doubt be supplied from the Constitution of the Presbyterian Church U.S.

Regarding the responsibilities of pastors, listed in the 1953 edition of *Presbyterian Law for the Local Church*,[1] Eugene Carson Blake cited the current Form of Government (G.IV), which defined the pastoral office in terms of biblical names: bishop, minister, presbyter, elder, and messenger of God. This "antique wording," Blake wrote, shows that it is there that the duties and rights of the pastor are indicated. He cites G.XVI.5, where it says that the pastor promises "to endeavor by the grace of God to adorn the profession of the gospel in his [her] manner of life and to walk with exemplary piety before the flock." The pastor also promises "to be faithful in the exercises of all . . . duties as a Christian and a minister of the gospel, whether personal or relative, private or public."

Indeed, in our contemporary *Constitution*, guidelines are spelled out with comparable specificity in sections where the responsibilities of church officers are defined.

- Church officers "should be persons of strong faith, dedicated discipleship, and love of Jesus Christ as Savior and Lord. Their manner of life should be a demonstration of the Christian gospel in the church and in the world. They must have the approval of God's people and the concurring judgment of a governing body of the church" (G-6.0106; also 6.0202 and .0303). Elders and deacons are particularly called upon to "perform by the law of love" (6.0304) and "be persons of spiritual character, honest repute, of exemplary lives, brotherly and sisterly love, warm sympathies and sound judgment" (6.0401).

- In a section dealing with the content of the vows that all church officers must take [see G-14.0405(2), (3), (5)], it is said to be necessary to the integrity and health of the church that officers adhere to the essentials of the Reformed faith and polity as expressed in the *Book of Confessions* and the Form of Government. Within these guidelines individuals have the right to exercise freedom of conscience, but this conscience must be "captive to the Word of God as interpreted in the standards of the church so long as he or she continues to seek or hold office in that body" (see G-6.0108). A pastor, furthermore, "is to be responsible for a quality of life and relationships that commend the gospel to all persons and that communicate its joy and its justice" (G-6.0202).

Questions for Study

1. *What are some examples of behavior that would be unbecoming for a Presbyterian officer?*
2. *People outside the church are often critical of Christian behavior and accuse us of being hypocrites. Is there any truth in this critique?*

Scriptural Guidance

All of our officers take a vow to accept the Scriptures as the unique and authoritative witness to Jesus Christ and God's Word to them (G-14.0801e(2), 14.0207b). But which texts from the Bible must be violated to constitute a breach of conduct? The former constitution of the United Presbyterian Church in the United States of America began with the Westminster standards and designated the Ten Commandments as the primary directives for Christian living. As the Larger Catechism puts it (Question 98), "The moral law is summarily comprehended in the Ten Commandments, which were delivered by the voice of God upon Mount Sinai." Although our understanding of the Decalogue has changed considerably since 1647, it would be difficult to find a better starting point to assess officers' conduct than to insist on their basic adherence to the worship of the one true God and to the admonitions against dishonoring parents, killing, committing adultery, stealing, bearing false witness, or coveting—commandments that are all summarized in Jesus' law of love (Mark 12:28–34 and parallels). Most Presbyterians would agree that these fundamental ethical guidelines are still valid for right living and Christ-centered ministry today.

In the New Testament, basic direction is found in 1 Peter 5:1–6 and related passages where service is defined in terms of shepherding (the scriptural word for pastoral leadership): "Tend the flock of God that is in your charge, exercising the oversight, not under compulsion but willingly, as God would have you do it—not for sordid gain but eagerly. Do not lord it over those in your charge, but be examples to the flock." This pastoral image is also applied to prophetic leadership in the Old Testament (Jer. 23:1–4; Ezek. 34:1–24; Zech. 11:15–17, etc.). Jesus similarly encourages his disciples to treat the people of God with special care and humility when he describes himself as the good shepherd (John 10:1–18; see Mark 10:35–45).

In 1 Timothy, furthermore, the church has a rich repository of moral and spiritual guidelines for church officers. In general, the author encourages leaders to maintain a strong belief system and a good conscience, warning that some have rejected conscience and suffered a shipwreck of their faith (1 Tim. 1:18–20). Later chapters give direct charges to those who hold specific offices, but it is usually understood today that most of these guidelines are useful to all officers, since the positions of bishop, deacon, and elder did not differ in rank and authority in the first century, but only in function and job description. The advice to a *bishop* to be above reproach, temperate, sensible, respectable, hospitable, an apt teacher, gentle, not quarrelsome, and a good manager of money is wise for anyone exercising authority in the church (1 Tim. 3:1–7). Admonitions to *deacons* to be serious, honest, not greedy, and to be good stewards of their own households, and the advice to *elders* to keep themselves free from partiality and to remain pure, are equally valid for all officers

(1 Tim. 3:8–12; 5:17–22). How spiritual leaders should conduct themselves is summarized well in 1 Timothy 4:12 and 6:11–14. Biblical passages about the nature of the sanctified life also provide valuable guideposts (see 1 Thess. 4:1–7; 5:12–22; Gal. 5:16–26). The concise Christocentric directive in Colossians 3:17 is often quoted at the end of ordination and installation services: "whatever you do, in word or deed, do everything in the name of the Lord Jesus, giving thanks to God . . . through him."

Presbyterians often complain that it is very difficult to determine the scriptural basis of conduct since there are so many different interpretations of the Bible as a whole and individual passages in particular. But we have no other choice. Believers are always forced to understand the Bible in the light of their own culture and current knowledge of biblical history and interpretation. The debates about circumcision in the New Testament, the arguments about the true nature of God prior to the Council of Nicaea in 325, the heated discussions today about evolution and creation, or the biblical perspectives about gay and lesbian lifestyles, all indicate that the church will always be struggling to understand the Bible correctly in every age. This ongoing quest for knowledge, however, should never deter us from using the Scriptures as the basis of our lives and ministries, even if our understanding is imperfect. They remain the primary guide for determining whether or not officers and pastors are worthy of their calling. (See the discussion regarding Ordination Vows, chapter 7.)

Questions for Study

1. *Read 1 Timothy 3:1–7. Which rules of conduct for church officers are especially important today?*
2. *Do you think that most church officers today can honestly say that they live according to the Ten Commandments?*

Being an Example

Those who have worked in the church for a length of time as church officers or pastors can usually count at least one satisfaction of service: they have been able to provide, if only in a small way, a positive example for those who are following them in ministry. It is a real joy in the midst of labor that can often be frustrating and lonely, to know that we have been able to help a few people strengthen their commitment and develop their skills in the service of the church of Christ.

Being a role model to others is more than a perquisite of church office. It is required of all those who would follow the scriptural and constitutional guidelines for the conduct of ministry (G-6.0106, D-2.0203). As 1 Peter 5:3 puts it, "Do not lord it over those in your charge, but be examples to the flock."

The Greek word *typos*, which we translate "example," is often used in the New Testament to direct church leaders. Paul teaches in a number of places that those in leadership positions have an obligation to do more than merely stay out of trouble. By their demeanor and deliberate behavior they must consciously set an example that others are proud to emulate (1 Thess. 1:7; 2 Thess. 3:9; Phil. 3:17).

In the pastoral epistles, as in 1 Peter, the authors wrote for a later set of circumstances when the church needed a more careful organizational structure. They ordered elders, deacons, and pastors to show others how to behave through their own careful comportment. "Set the believers an example in speech and conduct, in love, in faith, in purity" (1 Tim. 4:12). "Show yourself in all respects a model (*seauton parechomenos typon*) of good works, and in your teaching show integrity, gravity, and sound speech that cannot be censured" (Titus 2:7–8).

In other passages, New Testament authors make it clear that church leaders are to do more than provide passive role models. They are to be so bold as to urge others to "imitate" (from the Greek *mimeomai*) them in their ministries.

At the beginning of a new century we might be more modest or, knowing our mixed intentions, might even be reluctant to encourage anyone to be like us. But apostles and their successors were confident in the Spirit's power in their lives and were not shy about directing others to watch them closely and do as they were doing (1 Thess. 1:6; 1 Cor. 4:16, 11:1; Phil. 3:17). For this reason it is not surprising that one of the oldest parts of our *Constitution* (1797) urges us to consider the example of the apostles and the practice of the primitive church as authoritative (G-1.0400).

The early church leaders were not so assured, of course, merely because of their own abilities, but because they were imitating Jesus Christ and walking in his footsteps (1 Peter 2:21; Acts 20:35; 1 Cor. 11:1; 1 Tim. 1:16). Jesus himself told his disciples: "I have set you an example, that you should also do as I have done to you. Very truly, I tell you, servants are not greater than their master, nor are messengers greater than the one who sent them" (John 13:15–16; see G-6.0401). Thus it is no accident that one of the vows Presbyterian officers and leaders take is to seek to follow the Lord Jesus Christ in their own lives, and they should know that their ministry will be judged by how well they keep that promise (G-14.0405b(6)).

The standards of conduct for a church officer or pastor are placed on a high plane by the Scriptures and our *Constitution*. The examples we provide not only determine the quality of service where we work. They also powerfully influence those who are younger or less experienced than we are as they seek to develop their own spiritual and ethical guidelines in ministry.

We never know when others may be watching us as they try to decide how they should conduct themselves. If young people pay close attention to stars in professional sports to see what kind of behavior they should adopt, it is possible they might also be encouraged to observe pastors, elders, deacons, and others in the church to learn what they should be like when they are older. It is in this way that God helps all of us learn what it means to be a Christian. Others may watch how we succeed in the church; and they may especially be looking closely when we are under pressure, when we are criticized unfairly, or when we fail. Often you learn the most about dealing with conflict and stress when you see how others maintain professional composure in anxious times, love their enemies when they are attacked, and try to be ambassadors of Christ in all circumstances.

Questions for Study

1. *What does it mean to you personally to follow in the footsteps of Jesus?*
2. *Have you ever been disappointed by someone you looked up to as an example?*

Direction from the *Book of Confessions*

All officers at the time of ordination answer affirmatively when asked if they will be "instructed" and "guided" by the historic statements of faith found in the *Book of Confessions* [see G-14.0405b(3),(4)]. With this principle in mind, it is clear that one aspect of misconduct in ordained office involves actions that are contrary to directives found in the *Book of Confessions*.

What are some of these guidelines? The following passages provide a general orientation.[2]

The Scots Confession (1560). Certain actions separate believers from nonbelievers and are obviously particularly unacceptable among church leaders. Murderers, oppressors, cruel persecutors, adulterers, filthy persons, . . . thieves, all workers of iniquity, have neither the faith nor anything of the Spirit of the Lord Jesus Christ, so long as they continue in their wickedness. True believers fight against such behavior and rely on the power of Jesus to deliver them in the struggle of flesh against Spirit (C-3.13).

The Heidelberg Catechism (1563). The Ten Commandments are held up as basic ethical guidelines and their meaning is explored (C-4.092–.115). Also see the Shorter Catechism (1647, C-7.108). In the Larger Catechism the Decalogue is referred to as the place where the moral law is summarily comprehended (C-7.208).

The Second Helvetic Confession (1566). In a section that discusses the duties of ministers, pastors are encouraged to diligently see to everything that pertains to the tranquillity, peace, and welfare of the church; to be constantly in prayer, attend to spiritual reading, in all things to be watchful; and by purity of life to let their light shine before all people (C-5.163–.164). "At all times and in all places the rule is to be observed that everything is to be done for edification, decently and honorably, without oppression and strife" (C-5.165).

The Larger Catechism (1647)—In interpreting the Ten Commandments (the Fifth Commandment in particular), careful attention is paid to the obligations of superiors to inferiors (C-7.239–.240). Those who have authority over others are encouraged to love, pray for, and bless them; to instruct, counsel, and admonish them; to protect and provide for them all things necessary for soul and body; and by grave, wise, and holy example to procure glory to God and to themselves. The sins of those in authority include seeking power for themselves or their own glory, ease, profit, or pleasure; commanding unlawful things; counseling others in evil; discouraging them from doing good, or leading them to unjust, indiscreet, rigorous, or remiss behavior.

This text from the Larger Catechism provides a particularly powerful warning to those who exercise power in the church by virtue of their role or position. Professionals in the church need to be aware that some members will be drawn to them simply because they are seen as powerful public figures. It is always the responsibility of the pastor in counseling situations, or of any church officer at public and private meetings, youth group gatherings, or other places, to make certain nothing happens that could injure other members or themselves. The ordained person must take the initiative for controlling situations with members who are vulnerable, with young people, and with community members who are looking for support and love. The service of the church must be offered only in ethical and professional ways. If people who are served by the church exhibit inappropriate behavior (through transference or because of mental illness), the church officer must seek guidance and assistance. These may come from other officers or staff, from an executive presbyter, or from psychiatrists, psychologists, or social workers. It is the duty of the officer to make sure that the situation is corrected immediately and that the members in question receive appropriate pastoral care from other pastors or counselors. Situations where members mistakenly think the attention they are getting has sexual or personal overtones need to be helped. But at times it is necessary to protect officers and staff by finding other sources of care before great damage is done to individuals or to the congregation.

The Confession of 1967. One of our recent confessions focuses primarily on reconciliation through Christ between believers and God, and between Christians and the rest of the world. Presbyterian polity, this confession states, recognizes the responsibility of all members for ministry and it seeks to protect the church from exploitation from ecclesiastical or secular power or ambition (C-9.40). Church officers and members, therefore, are expected to receive and uphold one another in all areas of life: in employment, housing, education, leisure, marriage, and economics; to work against racial and sexual discrimination; and to avoid exclusion or domination of other people (C-9.44). The implication is clear: wherever church leaders or members deliberately breach God's purpose in achieving reconciliation in the world they violate their calling.

Although these confessional guidelines (along with others not mentioned here) need to be understood in their own historical contexts and must be interpreted in light of our culture and knowledge of Scripture, they provide the primary foundation for building the Reformed basis of professional and ethical standards for Presbyterian officers.

Questions for Study

1. Do you think that nominating committees and sessions consider the personal and ethical backgrounds of members before they ask them to become officers?

2. *If you knew that a church officer acted in prejudicial ways toward community members or exploited others economically, would you be in favor of trying to remove him or her from office? Do you think church officers should be censured if they are greedy, if they mistreat employees, if they are dishonest in their business dealings, or if they break the peace and unity of the church?*

Discipline as a Key Reformed Guideline

When Presbyterians think of discipline they usually have in mind the orderly exercise of administrative authority designed to correct behavior of offenders and preserve the unity of the church (D-Preamble, G-1.0300). Regarding the professional conduct of church officers, however, leading interpreters of Reformed principles of ministry point out that the kind of discipline that derives from personal adherence to scriptural, theological, and ethical rules is equally important.

As Jack Rogers puts it, discipline is as important to church leaders today as it is to athletes preparing for Olympic competition.[3] Life becomes more difficult and decision making becomes harder, rather than easier, when one becomes a Christian. And leaders especially need strength, preparedness, alertness, and all the abilities that discipline gives in order to the meet the challenges of contemporary Christian life. In today's church, he argues, we may too quickly look the other way when offenses are committed by clergy (this is true especially in regard to sexual harassment). Church members are vulnerable to the personal influence of leaders whom they trust, so officers must take their responsibilities with particular seriousness. Although ministers and other ordained officers have a right to have their own needs met, Rogers reminds us that we have responsibilities as well as rights. Our church "process of redress of grievances" makes sure we do not make excuses for conduct that could be avoided with the proper amount of discipline on the part of those who counsel and lead. "Freedom is compatible with the doctrine of election. And discipline is integral to the Reformed doctrine of the church."[4]

In a similar vein, John Leith points out that discipline has been a key moral and theological component for Reformed church leaders from the beginning.[5] Leaders must realize that the "doctrine of delayed satisfaction" provides the rationale for denying momentary pleasures for the sake of greater and more important long-range goals. That is, pastors and church officers must be prepared to think and act for themselves and not be swayed by contemporary moral standards as they face daily temptations. Preoccupation with the self and self-consciousness has undercut the disciplined Christian life. Personal discipline is often reduced merely to a matter of private choice, as public sanctions and supports are taken away. Leith hopes that a changed culture and political situation may make discipline a desired virtue again, helping leaders realize that "without it, the Reformed way of being a Christian is not possible."

As John Stott noted in an address to the Consultation of Preparation for Ministry in 1990, those who are called to ministry are given a directive by God to bear an alternate vision of what the world is to be or might be. They represent a word both of judgment and of promise, and are called to be "moral exemplars," different in some ways from the world as it is. "We who are ordained try at times to avoid this exemplary role. We know and confess our inadequacies and our misuse of our gifts and of our office. But the fact remains that leaders are called to exemplify those characteristics and virtues" that reflect the way they will lead others.[6]

Questions for Study

1. *Can you think of situations where you refused to bow to peer pressure and said "no" even when others mocked you for your conviction?*

2. *Part of discipline involves knowing the difference between right and wrong and committing only to the good. How hard is that to do if you are in business, in athletics, in education, in politics, or in entertainment?*

Testing the Standards

Presbyterians are sometimes put in a situation—by theological differences or by changes in society—where they must vigorously debate which course of action the church must take. But how will discussions take place when values are so different? When change seems to challenge the fundamental biblical and ethical assumptions of some of the members of the church, some basic questions may be in order.

1. Will congregations and presbyteries try to develop fair and honest discussions of the issues involved so that the Holy Spirit may work among brothers and sisters in faith, or will most members have their minds made up already? Will commissioners to presbytery meetings be allowed to vote their own consciences and follow the word of Christ, or will others put pressure on them to vote in predetermined ways, regardless of the fact that the *Constitution* forbids directing or intimidating them (G-1.0100b, .0300a, 4.0301d)?

2. When we explore the Scriptures again to determine what the Bible says about a controversial theological, ethical, or social issue, how will we know which opinions are correct when people express radically different interpretations? Is the evidence as obvious as biblical scholars (on both sides) claim, or can we still learn from further study and from each other? What are the eternal standards in Scripture? Which ones are "conditioned by the language, thought forms, and literary fashions of the places and times at which they were written" (Confession of 1967, C-9.29)?

3. Does being "reformed, always reforming" (G-2.0200) mean adherence to historic ethical principles or being open to growth and change under the direction of the Spirit? When is faith consistency necessary? When is it important to embrace change to avoid moral and spiritual deterioration and injustice?

4. How do we interpret the Scriptures and confessions when we know that some of the ethical demands in both are culturally determined and time bound? Some people argue that the

confessions do not offer valuable ethical guidelines because portions of them are outdated. Can we pick and choose what to believe? Do we have to take all or nothing? Do we have to accept historic theological directives that contradict the modern conscience? How do people in Reformed churches read the Bible and their confessions in light of history and scientific research?

5. Presbyterians have been free to change standards of ethics in the past. We no longer reject African Americans or women for ordination, although at one time some Christians argued that the Bible compelled us to do so on moral and scientific grounds. Prior to the early 1970s, pastors who were divorced and remarried were no longer allowed to serve churches because they were judged guilty of adultery. The church has changed its mind on this prohibition too. Is God calling for similar changes in cases that the church will be forced to examine in the future or will we be dealing with questions so different that these historical parallels are irrelevant?

6. How do we decide an issue in which the peace, unity, and purity of the church are at stake? If we have taken a vow to uphold these aspects of church life, what are our obligations to God, to the church, and to future generations as we study and debate issues of our day?

7. How significant is the evidence presented by medicine and science? Is it of less, more, or equal importance compared to the authority of Scripture, once we have correctly interpreted it (2 Tim. 2:15)?

8. When we make a decision, will it be consistent with one of the most spiritually centered directives in the Old Testament which calls us to justice: "What does the LORD require of you but to do justice, and to love kindness, and to walk humbly with your God" (Micah 6:8)? What does justice require?

9. As officers of the Presbyterian Church, we have all taken vows of obedience to Jesus Christ. What would he have us do in this case? Does his response to his disciples provide valuable guidelines? How do we apply the law of love here (love of God, love of neighbor, love of self)?

10. More personally, when you pray carefully and deeply about the questions being raised in the church, what does God say to you? What kind of attitude does God want you to adopt? When you pray, what do you discover about God's will? Is your attitude consistent with the best things we know about God's justice and mercy? Is it congruent with your own sense of calling?

Every generation of Presbyterians will have its own issues to test its faithfulness, wisdom, and willingness to change. Decisions about the issues that will be faced early in the twenty-first century will demonstrate who we are, what we believe, and what we think God is calling us to be. It will test our knowledge of Scripture, our theological acumen, our understanding of the Reformed tradition, and our ability to love one another. Let us pray for the wisdom to discover God's will with the hope that future generations will be able to look back on our debates and decisions and say that they are proud to be Presbyterians.

Chapter 9

Growing Your Church

The Choices

*I*f church officers in almost any congregation were able to sit around a table and make a list of the top objectives for the church in the next five years, most of them would inevitably say "we want to grow." If growth is to occur, however, we have to be committed to it and take the time to learn how it takes place. Along with the pastors and other staff, elders, deacons, and trustees are key people: without their support and active participation the congregation cannot move forward.

Why do churches want to grow? We know the answers already. Because we want to spread the gospel of Jesus Christ. Because we want to serve our communities and the world. Because we want to bring healing and love. Because we want the oppressed to have justice and freedom. Because we want equality and relief from the scourge of poverty.

Sometimes churches want to grow simply because they cannot survive without it. Facing the prospects of declining membership and worship attendance, many congregations know that if they do not take in new members (especially some younger ones) they will cease to exist. For them, it is grow or die.

Yet church growth involves more than strategies for getting additional people into the pews and strengthening the rolls. True growth in the body of Christ is also concerned with reaching out to current and lapsed members; developing spiritual growth through Bible study and prayer; examining the church's obligation to address local, national, and international ethical and political issues; increasing the participation of children and parents in church school; the development of stronger programs for teenagers; the nurturing of a deeper spiritual commitment to stewardship (including annual pledges as well as gifts to endowments); and active, hands-on growth in outreach and mission consciousness, coupled with a genuine sensitivity to peace and justice in the community and the world.

Simply listing all these aspects of church growth (and there are others) can be overwhelming for sessions and pastors. A few congregations may have the vitality and spiritual strength to attempt growth in all areas simultaneously, but for most churches, regardless of size and staffing patterns, growth inevitably involves very conscious, deliberate choices. If we want to encourage church growth, on which aspects do we focus? If we are in a growing suburb the answers will be different from those in a static residential area, a rural community where homes are far apart, or in the inner city, which has its own unique problems and opportunities.

A more fundamental choice also needs to be made. Do we really want to grow at all? Church growth, by its nature, will cause many changes and change is not only exciting but painful. New people bring in new ideas, demands, and expectations. Do we really want to alter our worship hours, adjust church school patterns, reach out to communities around us in love and justice? Can we endure if we try out new ministries and they fail? Are we willing to offer new programs and then find that no one attends them? Do we trust God enough to tolerate resistance to change and the resulting exasperation?

Questions for Study

1. *Which aspect of growth should your church embrace?*
2. *How will it change your life and ministry, and what costs will it bring to the community of faith and the individuals within it?*

Developing the Vision

For church growth there is a stage that must occur prior to planning in detail: the officers, staff, and congregation must be able to develop a vision, they must become or find the people who have the ability to hear the small, quiet voice of God, or at least resist the temptation to ignore the booming, unmistakable message of God. They must become or find members able to see ahead and anticipate where the ministry of Christ is going in the church and the community. This stage of church growth requires believers who are in tune with the Holy Spirit and have an intuitive sense about the future—those who have the spiritual gift of discernment (1 Cor. 2:15; 12:10)—and want to lead toward new horizons. Members who have more practical skills and are excellent at detailed planning and implementation (nuts and bolts) will be needed later; for now they may be required to simply listen and follow. The statement in Proverbs 29:18 is true, no matter how we translate it today: "Where there is no vision, the people perish" (KJV).

This part of church growth involves the creation of mission statements, goals, and objectives. But they need to be written in consultation with the whole congregation, the entire body of Christ in the local setting. One way to discover the needed information is to develop and distribute a *quantitative* survey containing questions to be answered by the members of the church. These are analyzed and then used to develop mission directions. Most pastors are familiar with instruments of this type. Forms of them may be obtained from presbytery executives or synod resource staff. It is also possible (and sometimes highly desirable) to develop the questions with the assistance of professional pollsters who can make sure the questionnaire is well written and the information collected is scientifically valid. Church-related organizations such as the Alban Institute[1] provide well-trained consultants who can assist congregations in assessing current systems and program areas and in examining and analyzing the beliefs and values of the membership.

A second method of obtaining information is the *qualitative* survey, which is often employed by businesses to initiate long-range planning. This instrument differs from the first because it does not use written questionnaires. Instead, questions are carefully developed and trained interviewers invite small groups to meet and discuss them. The consultations should always include time for participants to voice any opinions they want to share—in any form they wish to use: compliments for the programs and staff, concerns and gripes, hopes and dreams. In the Presbyterian Church, the groups selected might include the session, the deacons, trustees, Stephen Ministers, pastors and other staff, all major committees, and small groups of members (randomly called together). Opportunities are given to all members to participate in the process, and the responses are carefully recorded. With the assistance of professionals who are trained to weigh the information, an analysis is developed of significant trends, and drafts of a mission statement and goals and objectives are developed. After careful revision by the session and staff, they are presented to the congregation for examination, editing, and final approval.

Obviously the two survey instruments are not mutually exclusive—they may even be used in tandem to obtain the maximum amount of objective and subjective information. The General Assembly provides an excellent resource for churches looking for materials to enable them to begin this important discernment process. One book is particularly useful: *So What Is God Up to in Your World and Mine? A Resource Book for Leaders Doing Training in Congregational Development.*[2] It contains essays on the journey of faith; the image of God doing a new thing; the principles of Paul as a church founder and builder; redevelopment in the African American church; Bible studies on new partnerships that can lead the church into the twenty-first century; a redevelopment probe/exploration pilot project; along with an extensive bibliography. Loren Mead's books in the "Once and Future Church" series are especially valuable as guides for congregations trying to visualize the strategies that will be needed in the next fifty years.[3]

Questions for Study

1. *Has your congregation or presbytery participated in a self-study recently? What were the major conclusions?*
2. *Has your congregation or presbytery tried to assess what its goals for the future should be? What do you think they should be?*

Developing the Plan

Once the *choice* has consciously been made for a congregation to grow, and once leaders and members of the church have received a *vision* that can be expressed in a general mission statement, the time comes when detailed *plans* for church growth may be developed. Some of the steps include (not necessarily in this order) the following:

1. In a preliminary phase, local or county agencies and presbytery and synod resources may be consulted to obtain the most recent demographic information about the area in which the church is found. Demographic, ethnographic, psychographic, praxiographic, and mediagraphic studies provide necessary statistics about the age, location, family size, and various religious and cultural preferences of people in the community around the church.[4] What is discovered will impact the shape of future programs. If the median age in the community is thirty-four, a ministry is called for that is quite different than one required where the age is sixty-four. A community with burgeoning school systems requires programs unlike those needed in one that is not growing or is marked by an increase in retirement housing.

2. Estimates need to be made of financial resources that will be available and how additional funds will be raised. Studies of past giving patterns and average annual pledge increases, along with possible income from endowment principal and interest income, will all need to be carefully made. Possible loans from higher governing bodies and lending institutions may also be considered.

The staff and materials provided by the Church Financial Campaign Service of the Presbyterian Church (U.S.A.) are able to assist congregations of any size. Their expert campaign directors provide the practical and spiritual direction and stewardship resources to enable congregations to set and reach fund-raising goals. They stay in close contact with staff and committee members, and because of long years of experience they are able to tailor a campaign program to suit particular needs and circumstances.[5]

3. At this stage, a second set of meetings with the session, other boards, major committees, social groups, staff, and the congregation is needed. One way to proceed is to ask each major committee and group within the church to develop long-range plans in their areas of ministry that are congruent with the mission statement previously approved by the session and the congregation.

Although *goals* that are finally adopted may be general in nature, *objectives* need to be specific and measurable so they are obtainable and may be evaluated later. The statement of goals and objectives for spiritual development might look like this.

Goal
To increase the spiritual growth of church members over the next five years.

Objectives
1. To offer three new Bible study series each year
2. To develop and continue a midweek contemporary service of worship
3. To write five new hymns to be used in services of worship

If building programs are involved in projected plans, the town, city, and county offices need to be consulted about local building requirements or restrictions if the church is listed on the National Register of Historic Sites. Contact also needs to be made with the trustees or appropriate committee of presbytery to receive valuable advice and necessary presbytery approval of plans to borrow money or encumber or purchase real property (G-8.0500).

At this point, initial proposals may be drawn up in consultation with architects, interior designers, and landscapers. Estimates of project budgets and long-range funding requirements for continuing maintenance are made. Fund-raising plans and schedules are organized and a flow chart of activities is drafted and approved by session. Once these plans are in place they need to be discussed during a third round of meetings with appropriate groups and committees before they are finally approved by session and the congregation. Although three sets of discussions may seem excessive and time-consuming, proposals that are not openly debated and accepted by the majority of the members during the early steps may ultimately fail for lack of enthusiasm and support. What is more, staff and session should desire the maximum amount of feedback and information available from formal and informal groups within the congregation. Members of the church are going to provide the volunteer support and the money for any programs for church growth. They also know the community well, understand their neighbors's hopes and needs, and support the program with the power of their prayers. To put it simply: church growth programs that utilize a patronizing, trickle-down kind of formulation (that is, starting at the top with staff or leading officers) do not usually catch fire. It is far more effective and far more satisfying to want information and support from the congregation, and to use it when it is given.

This final stage of planning requires not only careful selection of committee chairpersons and committee members to assure the highest quality of leadership, but also regular and careful reporting to the session, trustees, staff, and congregation as the program proceeds.

5. Any specific plans which are developed for church growth need to include long-range goals and objectives for mission and outreach. No doubt outreach will be at the heart of the church's mission statement from the beginning. At this point the outreach or mission committee can work with the congregation to develop specific objectives and budgets for the next few years. In one

church in which I served, it seemed that local and world needs in mission were so huge that we wanted to help everyone at once. Yet we knew we had to focus our energies if we were to accomplish anything of substance. Thus, after considerable study and prayer, we decided to fund local programs that worked against violence and fostered peacemaking. On the international front, we concentrated on Presbyterian mission in Africa, especially in two or three regions of Ethiopia. Because we limited our choices, our goals and objectives were clear and were more easily defined, interpreted, and evaluated.

Concentrating on mission is crucial for the continuing spiritual growth of the church. As Christians we know we are called to reach out in love to the local community, the nation, and the world in Christ's love. We are called to witness and to bring healing and justice to the weak, oppressed, and marginalized. Many congregations decide at the beginning of a fund-raising campaign to designate a significant proportion of the pledges to mission (often 20–50 percent), knowing that the church will grow in proportion to its desire to follow Christ and do his work. The old adage is true: churches do not collapse because they give too much away; they die because they try to keep their love, money, and energy all to themselves.

This detailed stage of church growth is not one that needs to be divorced from the spiritual work of the church. Solomon reminded the people of Israel that all plans for the building of the Temple should develop out of the calling of the people of God: to allow them to keep covenant and steadfast love with their Creator; to build a place where God's name will always be present; to give the people a sanctuary where the watchwords will be integrity before God and the gift of forgiveness and aid to those oppressed and excluded by society (1 Kings 8:22–53). Their planning, the king reminds them, is designed to create a center where God will always be with them and a place where they will incline their hearts to God's ways, so that all the people of the earth will know that the Lord is God and there is no other (1 Kings 8:57–60).

For congregations entering this stage in church growth, an

exciting experience awaits. Every church is a living organism and leaders have a responsibility to discover the way God wants the body to grow and develop. What we are trying to accomplish requires boldness and faith: both to ascertain where Christ intends to be in the future and to be prepared to meet him there. No matter how we plan for this growth we need to keep the ultimate vision before us. If true spiritual development is to occur, those attempting to determine God's will must depend on the Head of the body to lead where we must go. As Paul says when discussing leadership principles for the Corinthian church, "I planted, Apollos watered, but God gave the growth" (1 Corinthians 3:6).

Questions for Study

1. *If you cannot do everything, how can you discover what you can do?*
2. *How do you decide if the choice involves two good things? How do you decide between one bad thing and one good thing? What do you do if you are forced to choose between two bad things? How do you know the difference?*

Counting the Cost

Sometimes when congregations are making plans for church growth they stop after the first three stages, before the process is complete. This is a mistake, because it often costs the church money and slows forward momentum when it is discovered later that plans were not detailed enough to ensure that they could be implemented. As Jesus warned, before a man builds a tower he counts the cost (Luke 14:26–32).

1. Counting all the costs

If a church decides to make its building handicapped accessible, officers need to be certain that all of the costs have been taken into account. If an elevator will be installed, the choice of size and capacity will be determined by its use. Will it only be used for people or will the church need it to transport tables, chairs, television and VCR stands, handbell cases, etc.? When the cost is considered, has adequate provision been made in the annual budget to pay for monthly inspections and the fee for the emergency phone line that must be installed in the cab? Often it is assumed, even without thinking, that maintenance costs of new equipment will magically be absorbed by the annual budget. But if pledges are static, what will be cut to absorb these new expenses? Who will run the elevator during peak use? How can it be protected from abuse?

Other ramifications must also be considered. If a church is handicapped accessible, wonderful opportunities for evangelism and new member growth may develop. The session needs to consider other questions, however. If more senior citizens use the building, will new programs for them need to be introduced? If new members with multiple handicaps ask for other services, how willing will the congregation be to change? Is it possible to alter the worship space to meet their needs (perhaps pews should be removed to allow more room for wheel chair access) and to make them feel truly welcomed? Can you afford to install electronic equipment for the hearing or sight impaired?

One method of counting the cost of new construction used by many nonprofit organizations is to put money in escrow to maintain new buildings and equipment. Formulas may differ, but the session might decide, for example, that construction will not start until enough money is pledged to cover the cost of construction, *plus* funds equaling 20 percent more. This extra money could be placed in a restricted endowment that allows only the interest to be used for maintenance expenses.

Other hidden costs of construction and program development also must be considered. If a new copier is installed with two-sided copying, sorting, and stapling, how is this equipment going to be maintained? Is provision made for upgrading or purchasing new computers every three years or so, as the needs for speed, RAM, and Internet capability increase? If a local-area network (LAN) or a voice mail phone system is installed, where will money come from to service them or to make needed software adjustments? Will the new equipment require the hiring of more staff, or will it simply enable the current staff to be more efficient, or even make it possible to reduce the number of employees in the office?

Costs also have to be considered when new programs are introduced. Many churches are currently adding services of worship (often with a contemporary flair) in order to give members more flexibility and to attract new worshipers. But all the factors must be calculated. Will a new service require increased salaries for the organist and choir director? Will it mean that choir members will provide music for more services? Will they need more rehearsal time? Which volunteers will usher? Who will provide coffee and cookies for the fellowship hour? If the sanctuary is used more often, will it take more of the custodian's time? Is she or he expected to provide this service for free? What about the pastor's commitment? Most pastors are already working with an overburdened schedule. Can a new service be added without causing fatigue, resentment, or burnout? If the pastor's schedule is cut back in other areas to make time for this service, will the congregation really respect the change, or will they demand that nothing be cut out at all?

2. Midterm evaluation

Once programmatic changes have been made and new construction has been completed, it is necessary, about halfway through the five-year process, to assess what has happened thus far. Which goals and objectives are on track? Which ones are already completed? (Perhaps the new youth program took off like a rocket and is already fully functioning!) Which ones are not even in the planning stage yet? Are there any that now appear (after some time has passed) to have been bad ideas from the beginning? Is it time to scrap them or do they simply need to be reworked?

Midterm evaluation also allows the church to adjust to changing situations. Since the initial stages for long-range planning

occur years before programs are implemented, it is likely that
new opportunities will come along that never could have been
anticipated. One of the exciting things about being part of the
body of Christ is that we do not and will not know everything
that is coming next. Often pastors, church officers, and sessions
serve God on a "need to know basis." When we need to know
what is coming next, God will let us know, and not before.

Once when I served a church in northern New York state, we
went through a careful process of planning. But there was no
way we could have anticipated that refugees from Central America would be moving into our area, and we never could have
guessed that we would have homeless families living in our
church building, or that the whole community would become
responsible for the welfare of hundreds of people waiting for
visas to move into Canada.

One of our responsibilities as prayerful Christians is to be so
close to God in Christ, and to be in touch with the Holy Spirit on
such an intimate basis, that when new orders come from the
Chief, we will be spiritually mature enough and open enough to
recognize them as God's will for us in a changing situation.

3. Starting the process again

Near the end of the fourth year of a long-range plan (or sometime in the fifth year), the process of church growth and futuring
needs to begin again. By then, many of the goals and objectives
will have been reached. The local community may have
changed, members may have come and gone, and staff members
may have moved on. Now the time will come when the church
must be able to hear a new word from the Lord and be prepared
to develop a new vision and new plans.

Church growth and long-range planning are part of an exciting spiritual process. It requires the many varied talents and
skills of all the members of the church—spiritual discernment,
perceiving God's will, developing a heart to serve the community and the world, building God's house in a myriad of practical ways, and being open to the ongoing, reforming work of the

Spirit in our midst. Being responsible stewards involves continually strengthening the church for ministry. It includes anticipating a time, acknowledging a time, and building for a time when those doing the planning will no longer be there: knowing that whenever that time comes, the same God who leads us now, will guide church members into a future now being designed for them.

Questions for Study

1. How closely should a vision of the future be connected to practical finances?
2. Does prayer have the power to change what you can afford to do?

Making Important Decisions in Your Church and in Your Life

All Christians are forced to make critical decisions in their private lives and in the course of the development of their extended families. Church officers have the added burden of making critical choices for congregations and higher governing bodies that may impact many people for generations to come.

But how do we know what God's will is when we are making major decisions for ourselves or for the church? A shorthand process may help those who are not sure how to proceed. The basic elements include future considerations, financial needs and goals, family concerns, and the discernment of God's will through intuition, prayer, and spiritual advice.

Future

Regarding goals for the future, for example, a pastor or church officer considering a job move should ask several questions. Where do I want to be in five years? Is this move or decision consistent with my professional goals or with the long-range goals of the church? What are the opportunities? What are the obstacles? What are the advantages or disadvantages? If I turn down the job or if the church (or company) does not decide in my favor, what are the losses? Will this kind of opportunity come again or will the window close? Are the gains greater or smaller if I accept the risk?

Financial

A second consideration involves financial analysis. What is the old salary vs. the new salary? Will the living costs be more or less? If we build the addition, put in the elevator, or buy the new organ, can we afford the maintenance and new salaries involved? What costs are involved in moving, selling, or buying houses or hiring architects? Is it more expensive to fix up what we have or tear down and rebuild? Jesus knew that these were important practical questions. Before going to war, the king must count the cost (Luke 14:31–32).

Family and personal

As Christians we often say that our families are very important to us, and indeed loved ones should be foremost in our minds when we make decisions. A pastor might ask how a move will impact his or her family? How will it influence the spiritual and intellectual growth of children? Will it affect their financial future? What will the move do to you as a husband, wife, mother, father, or as a person? Will it make you easier or harder to live with? How will it influence your time, your "being there" for the rest of the family?

If the decision involves a congregation, we might ask if the body has the physical and spiritual energy to carry it out? Are there enough volunteers to carry out a new program? Will its introduction create too much stress in the lives of those who must work on it? Will it pull parents away from their children; will it take energy away from other important functions in the church?

Was the decision process fair and open, or are there too many hurt or angry feelings in the wake of the change? Will the decision make the atmosphere in the church better or worse? One of my wise elders once said, when he was advising me to back off an issue I was strongly supporting, "Remember, you can't push a rope uphill!"

Intuition and prayer

Church members do not always value intuition highly enough. Studying pros and cons, planning, and setting long-range goals are all very important and we must use them, but often we do not rely on the "gut feelings" of those who are most intimately involved with the decision. God can work through the intuition of spiritually wise people, and usually does. Despite all the rational reasons in the world, if a decision still *feels* wrong, it may be just that. On other occasions, if intuition tells us that a step forward or a call is right, that may be the only reason we finally need.

God works primarily through the inner person (Eph. 3:16–19). What do we learn through prayer about the decision? What does intuition tell us? What do spiritually wise people, whom you trust and love, tell you is best? Is this decision-making process in accord with the way other Christians have made decisions throughout the centuries? Ignatius of Loyola (1491–1556) provides four criteria by which choices may be made.[6] As he puts it, the time to make a decision is when "God our Lord moves and attracts the will in such a way that a devout person, without doubting or being able to doubt, carries out what was proposed."[7]

Does your decision affect your integrity, your morality, your most basic principles—what makes you, you? Is this decision entirely honest? Will it support peace and justice, or will it lead to pain or oppression for other people? Does it stand positively against the most critical Christian judgment, so that whatever you do in word or deed, everything can be done in the name of Jesus Christ, our Lord (Col. 3:17)?

Conclusions

In your final decision are you basically at peace? Does it create what Ignatius calls "tranquillity," a period "when the soul is not being moved one way or the other by various spirits and uses its natural faculties in freedom and peace"?[8] If all four areas of examination result in an affirmative answer, are you ready to make a decision? If not, set a deadline when the decision can be made.

After the decision is made, and you think it is what God wants, do not keep looking back. Assume it is right, and look for the reasons in the future that affirm the wisdom of God's direction. Write down the positive factors that led you to your decision and review them later when "buyer's remorse" inevitably sets in. Above all, when you know you have chosen wisely, get on with life, respect your decision, and trust God.

Notes

Items marked PDS or OGA are available from Presbyterian Distribution Service, 100 Witherspoon St., Louisville, KY 40202-1396 (phone: 800-524-2612; e-mail: *orders@pcusa.org*; Web site: *http://apps.pcusa.org/PDS/index.html*).

CHAPTER 1: BEING A CHURCH OFFICER

1. Joan S. Gray and Joyce C. Tucker, *Presbyterian Polity for Church Officers,* 3d ed. (Louisville, Ky.: Geneva Press, 1999), 29–30.

2. For discussions of the history of the development of church offices see H. J. Carpenter, "Minister, Ministry," in *A Theological Word Book of the Bible,* ed. Alan Richardson (New York: Macmillan Co., 1950); Edward Schillebeeckx, *Ministry: Leadership in the Community of Jesus Christ* (New York: Crossroad, 1981).

3. *Pastoral Expectations Inventory* (New York: United Presbyterian Church in the U.S.A., 1976).

4. *Manual for Church Officers and Members, of the Government, Discipline, and Worship of the Presbyterian Church in the United States of America,* 16th ed. (Philadelphia: Office of the General Assembly, 1950), 322–23.

5. Gray and Tucker, *Presbyterian Polity for Church Officers,* 146.

6. Oswald Chambers, *My Utmost for His Highest: An Updated Version in Today's Language,* ed. James Reimann (Grand Rapids: Discovery House Publications, 1992), reading for August 5.

7. See Roy M. Oswald, *Running through the Thistles: Terminating a Ministerial Relationship with a Parish* (Washington, D.C.: Alban Institute, 1978); Edward A. White, *Saying Goodbye: A Time of Growth for Congregations and Pastors* (Washington, D.C.: Alban

Institute, 1990); Herb Miller, "When Should I Say Goodbye?" *Net Results* (April 1996), 4–13.

CHAPTER 2: QUESTIONS OFFICERS OFTEN ASK

1. Congregations with less than seventy members may chose to elect a smaller nominating committee (G-14.0201c).

2. It is also possible for the session to call a special congregational meeting to fill incomplete terms.

3. For other resources about the work of a nominating committee see:

Joan S. Gray and Joyce C. Tucker, *Presbyterian Polity for Church Officers*, 3d ed. (Louisville, Ky.: Geneva Press, 1999), 25–28.

Frank A. Beattie, *Companion to the Constitution: Polity for the Local Church,* 4th ed. (Louisville, Ky.: Geneva Press, 1996), 55–62.

Edward K. Trefz, *Nominating Church Officers*, revised by W. Ben Lane (PDS #0640001).

William H. Venable, *Your Job as a Church Officer: A Manual for Officers of the Local Presbyterian (U.S.A.) Congregation* (Pittsburgh: Rivertree Christian Ministries, 12th printing, 1998).

Eugene D. Witherspoon, Jr., and Marvin Simmers, eds., *Called to Serve: A Workbook for Training Nominating Committees and Church Officers* (Louisville, Ky.: Curriculum Publishing, Presbyterian Church (U.S.A.), 1997).

For further nominating materials and officer training materials from the Presbyterian Church (U.S.A.) and other sources see *Guide to Resources (1999–2000)*, PDS #70358-99-001, which contains resources available from Presbyterian Distribution Service.

CHAPTER 3: THE PRINCIPLES BEHIND THE *BOOK OF ORDER* AND THE FORM OF GOVERNMENT

1. John Calvin, *Institutes of the Christian Religion*, ed. John T. McNeill, trans. Ford Lewis Battles (Philadelphia: Westminster Press, 1960), 4.3.10. See the discussion of Calvin's concept of order in church government by David B. McCarthy, "The Emerging Importance of Presbyterian Polity," in *The Organizational Revolution: Presbyterians and American Denominationalism*, ed. Milton J Coalter, John M. Mulder, and Louis B. Weeks (Louisville, Ky.: Westminster/John Knox Press, 1992), 303–5.

2. Calvin, *Institutes*, 4.10.27.

3. Calvin, *Institutes*, 4.10.30. For Calvin's contribution to the Presbyterian sense of order see *The Nature of the Church and the*

Practice of Governance (approved by the 205th General Assembly (1993) of the Presbyterian Church (U.S.A.), published by the Office of the General Assembly, 1993), 11–14; John H. Leith, *An Introduction to the Reformed Tradition: A Way of Being the Christian Community* (Atlanta: John Knox Press, 1981), chapter 5, "Polity and the Reformed Tradition," 145–73.

4. Lewis L. Wilkins, Jr., "The American Presbytery in the Twentieth Century," in *The Organizational Revolution*, 98.

5. Wilkins, "The American Presbytery," 98.

6. For a time line of constitutional history in the United States see *Manual for Church Officers and Members,* 17–22. Also see appropriate notes in *Book of Order, Presbyterian Church (U.S.A.), Annotated Edition, 1999–2000*. Available from Presbyterian Distribution Service, #OGA-99-013.

7. McCarthy, "Presbyterian Polity," in *Organizational Revolution,* 281–82, 306, points out the tendency in the last few years to solve issues of denominational identity through polity rather than theological debate, despite the apparent theological merit of the questions involved.

8. McCarthy, "Presbyterian Polity," 303–6.

9. *Manual for Church Officers and Members*, 38–39.

10. See the *1999–2000 Presbyterian Planning Calendar*, PDS #70-350-99-500, available from Presbyterian Distribution Service; and see the resource book published by Witherspoon Press, *The Great Ends of the Church: Worship Resources for Congregations*.

11. Joint Report of the Office of the General Assembly, the General Assembly Council, the Presbyterian Publishing Corporation, the Presbyterian Church (U.S.A.) Foundation, the Board of Pensions, and the Presbyterian Investment and Loan Program, Inc., *Minutes, 209th General Assembly, 1997*, Part I, *Journal* (Louisville, Ky.: Office of the General Assembly, 1997), 203.

12. *Presbyterian Law for the Local Church: A Handbook for Church Officers and Members*, ed. Eugene Carson Blake (Philadelphia: Published for the Office of the General Assembly by the Publication Division of the Board of Christian Education, 1953), 14. Also see the discussion of these principles in *The Nature of the Church and the Practice of Governance*, 14–17.

13. For a discussion of the way these principles applied to churches before they formed together as a denomination, see "The Organizational Revolution: Denomination and Leadership," in *The Re-Forming Tradition: Presbyterians and Mainstream Protestantism*, by Milton J Coalter, John M. Mulder, and Louis B. Weeks, (Louisville, Ky.: Westminster/John Knox Press, 1992), 91–96.

14. *Book of Order, Presbyterian Church (U.S.A.), Annotated Edition, 1999–2000* (Louisville, Ky.: Office of the General Assembly, PC(USA), 1999). Presbyterian Distribution Service, #OGA-99-013.

15. For further discussion see Gray and Tucker, *Presbyterian Polity for Church Officers*, 116; Frank A. Beattie, *Companion to the Constitution: Polity for the Local Church*, 4th ed. (Louisville, Ky.: Geneva Press, 1996), 55–62.

CHAPTER 4: IN THE SPIRIT: THE DIRECTORY FOR WORSHIP

1. *Book of Common Worship*, Prepared by The Theology and Worship Ministry Unit (Louisville, Ky.: Westminster/John Knox Press, 1993).

2. For information about the background see Ronald P. Byars, "Challenging the Ethos: A History of Presbyterian Worship Resources in the Twentieth Century," in *The Confessional Mosaic: Presbyterians and Twentieth-Century Theology*, ed. Milton J Coalter, John M. Mulder, and Louis B. Weeks (Louisville, Ky.: Westminster/John Knox Press, 1990), 134–61; Gray and Tucker, *Presbyterian Polity for Church Officers,* 160–75; C. Benton Kline, *A Study Guide for the Directory for Worship* (Louisville, Ky.: Presbyterian Publishing House, 1990).

3. *Book of Common Worship*, 13. It is also available in software in Macintosh and Windows versions from Westminster John Knox Press. For discussions about the purposes of the *Book of Common Worship* and analyses of its strengths see David Hoyt Pfleiderer, "Are We Getting Too Much Ritual in Our Presbyterian Worship?" *Presbyterian Outlook*, August 2–9, 1993, p. 8; Donald Wilson Stake, "The *Book of Common Worship* 1993," *Presbyterian Outlook*, September 6, 1993, p. 6; Catherine Gunsalus González, "The Book of Common Worship: A Theological Perspective," *Presbyterian Outlook*, September 20, 1993, p. 5.

4. *The Worshipbook—Services and Hymns* (Philadelphia: Westminster Press, 1972).

5. *The Presbyterian Hymnal—Hymns, Psalms and Spiritual Songs* (Louisville, Ky.: Westminster/John Knox Press, 1990); also available in a software edition on CD-ROM from Westminster John Knox Press.

6. *The Presbyterian Hymnal*, 9.

7. Daniel B. Wessler, "Why a New Directory Now?" *Reformed Liturgy and Music* 23, no. 4 (1989): 174 .

8. C. Benton Kline, "The New Directory for Worship on the Use of Language," *Reformed Liturgy and Music* 23, no. 4 (1989): 190.

9. Oswald Chambers, *My Utmost for His Highest,* reading for October 17.

10. Leslie D. Weatherhead, *A Private House of Prayer* (Nashville: Abingdon Press, 1958, 1979).

11. John Calvin, *Instruction in Faith (1537),* trans. Paul T. Fuhrmann (1949; Louisville, Ky: Westminster/John Knox Press, 1992), 68.

12. Calvin, *Institutes of the Christian Religion,* 4.14.2.

13. See *The Liturgy of the Church of Scotland since the Reformation,* Part I, *Calvin's Liturgy at Strasburg and Geneva,* ed. Stephen A. Hurlbut (Washington, D.C.: St. Albans Press, 1944), 19–20.

14. The author found this reference in the session records of the West Charlton United Presbyterian Church, West Charlton, New York. The ironic thing was that the lyrics, which one member heard coming out of another member's kitchen window, were repeated verbatim in the record!

15. See William D. Maxwell, *A History of Worship in the Church of Scotland* (London: Oxford University Press, 1955), 173–75.

16. Children were admitted to the table for first time in 1970. Prior to that they had to wait until they were confirmed.

17. See, however, PDS #74292-97-002, *Respectful Presence: An Understanding of Interfaith Prayer, Celebration and Worship from a Reformed Perspective,* and PDS #74292-94-903, *Being Ecumenical: A Compendium on Ecumenical and Interfaith Relations,* ed. Margaret O. Thomas. Also see *Presbyterian Principles for Interfaith Dialogue,* PDS #74-292-99-002.

18. For some additional resources to assist in understanding Presbyterian and Reformed traditions of worship see the following:

Cynthia Campbell and J. Frederick Holper, *Praying in Common,* Presbyterian Distribution Service, Keynote addresses presented at the Festivals of Worship introducing the *Book of Common Worship,* PDS #70420-94-200.

Following Christ Today: Reformed Spirituality, Videotape, PDS #041088.

Gray and Tucker, *Presbyterian Polity for Church Officers,* "Leading the Church in Worship," 170–87.

Donald L. Griggs, *In Spirit and in Truth: The Directory for Worship,* Videotape with a *Leader's Guide* (Merchantville, N.J.: Interlink Video Productions, 1991).

Howard G. Hageman, *Pulpit and Table: Some Chapters in the History of Worship in the Reformed Churches* (Richmond: John Knox Press, 1962).

LindaJo H. McKim, *The Presbyterian Hymnal Companion* (Louisville, Ky.: Westminster/John Knox, 1993).

Hughes Oliphant Old, *Worship That Is Reformed according to Scripture*, Guides to the Reformed Tradition, ed. John H. Leith and John W. Kuykendall (Atlanta: John Knox Press, 1984).

Reformed Liturgy and Music, a quarterly journal that includes practical aids for preaching, book reviews, and perspectives on hymns and music. Order from the Office of Theology and Worship, 100 Witherspoon St., Louisville, KY 40202-1396.

Howard Rice, *Reformed Spirituality* (Louisville, Ky.: Westminster/John Knox Press, 1991), especially 71–94 and 177–200.

William S. Smith, *Hymnsearch: Indexes for The Presbyterian Hymnal*, 1995. Address all inquiries to the author, 1826 Ridgeover Place, Jackson, MS 39211.

Donald Wilson Stake, *The ABCs of Worship: A Concise Dictionary* (Louisville, Ky.: Westminster/John Knox Press, 1992).

Bard Thompson, *Liturgies of the Western Church* (Cleveland: Meridian Books, 1961).

"Through Jesus Christ: Worship and Faith," Videotape, Presbyterian Distribution Service, PDS #076908.

CHAPTER 5: DEALING WITH CONFLICT IN THE CHURCH: THE RULES OF DISCIPLINE

1. *Manual for Church Officers and Members*, 16th ed. (Philadelphia: Office of the General Assembly, 1950), 135.

2. John Calvin, *Institutes of the Christian Religion*, 4.12.1.

3. *Institutes of the Christian Religion*, 4.12.1.

4. *Institutes of the Christian Religion*, 4.12.2.

5. *Institutes of the Christian Religion*, 4.12.5.

6. *Institutes of the Christian Religion*, 4.12.7.

7. Howard L. Rice, *Reformed Spirituality*, 122.

8. *Reformed Spirituality*, 123. For a more detailed study of Calvin's concepts of discipline and polity see John H. Leith, *An Introduction to the Reformed Tradition* (Atlanta: John Knox Press, 1977, 1981), chapter 5, "Polity and the Reformed Tradition."

9. James W. Angell, *How to Spell Presbyterian*, rev. ed. (Philadelphia: Geneva Press, 1984), 59, 60.

10. *Presbyterian Law for the Local Church*, 80–81.

11. *The Nature of the Church and the Practice of Governance,* 3–4; #OGA-93-01 /.

12. *The Nature of the Church and the Practice of Governance,* 29–30.

13. *The Nature of the Church and the Practice of Governance,* 31.

14. *Office of the General Assembly Online,* on the Web page for the Presbyterian Church (U.S.A.), www.pcusa.org/oga, "Potential Dangers in Certain Actions of Dissent," Policy Reflections, note 17, December 11, 1997.

15. Policy Reflections, note 17, p. 4.

16. Policy Reflections, note 17, pp. 4–5.

17. See, for example, chapter 14 in Beattie, *Companion to the Constitution,* "When There Is Conflict in the Particular Church," 165–72, where the five types and levels of conflict are defined and resources for dealing with them are outlined. For a basic introduction see Hugh F. Halverstadt, *Managing Church Conflict* (Louisville, Ky.: Westminster/John Knox Press, 1991).

18. Edwin H. Friedman, *Generation to Generation: Family Process in Church and Synagogue* (New York and London: Guilford Press, 1985), 208–10.

19. The record of cases heard by the General Assembly Permanent Judicial Commission and their results or verdicts are recorded each year in the *Minutes of the General Assembly,* Part I, *Journal,* in the part of the Office of the General Assembly report entitled "Matters Related to the Permanent Judicial Commission."

20. *The Nature of the Church and the Practice of Governance,* 29.

CHAPTER 6: THE *BOOK OF CONFESSIONS*: A THUMBNAIL SKETCH

1. Arthur C. Cochrane, *Reformed Confessions of the 16th Century* (Philadelphia: Westminster Press, 1966), 16–17.

2. For studies of the historic confessions of other churches including those found in Roman Catholic, Lutheran, evangelical, and free church traditions, see Ted A. Campbell, *Christian Confessions, A Historical Introduction* (Louisville, Ky.: Westminster John Knox Press, 1996). Also see *The Nature of Confession: Evangelicals and Postliberals in Conversation,* ed. Timothy R. Phillips and Dennis L. Okholm (Downers Grove, Ill.: InterVarsity Press, 1996). For further study of other Reformed confessions, see Jan Rohls, *Reformed Con-*

fessions: Theology from Zurich to Barmen (Louisville, Ky.: Westminster John Knox Press, 1998). A recent helpful tool is Joel R. Beeke and Sinclair B. Ferguson, eds., *Reformed Confessions Harmonized: With an Annotated Bibliography of Reformed Doctrinal Works* (Grand Rapids: Baker Books, 1999).

3. Edward A. Dowey, Jr., *A Commentary on the Confession of 1967 and an Introduction to The Book of Confessions* (Philadelphia: Westminster Press, 1968), 32–33.

4. John H. Leith, *Creeds of the Churches: A Reader in Christian Doctrine from the Bible to the Present* (New York: Doubleday & Co., Anchor Books, 1963), 3.

5. "The Confessional Nature of the Church," in Donald K. McKim, *Major Themes in the Reformed Tradition* (Grand Rapids: Wm. B. Eerdmans Publishing Co., 1992), 25–26.

6. Dowey, *A Commentary on the Confession of 1967*, 30. For additional reading see:

Perky Daniels, "What Presbyterians Believe: Why Do We 'Confess' Our Faith?" *Presbyterians Today*, June 1996, 17–19.

Harry W. Eberts, Jr., *We Believe: A Study of the Book of Confessions for Church Officers* (Philadelphia: Geneva Press, 1987).

J. W. Greg Meister, *To All Generations: The Book of Confessions*, Videotape (Interlink Video Productions, Inc., P.O. Box 1004, Merchantville, NJ 01809).

Jack Rogers, *Presbyterian Creeds* (Louisville, Ky.: Westminster/John Knox Press, 1991 (complete)). (First published 1985; supplement in 1991.)

7. See Jack L. Stotts and Jane Dempsey Douglass, *To Confess the Faith Today* (Louisville, Ky.: Westminster/John Knox Press, 1990); Rogers, *Presbyterian Creeds*. Also see Jack Rogers's videotapes: "Touring the Creeds" and "Introduction to a New Brief Statement of Faith" (Essential Media Services, 629 Garfield Pl., Arroyo Grande, CA 93420).

8. See Clarice Martin, "Inclusive Language and the Brief Statement of Faith: Widening the Margins in Our Common Confession," in Stotts and Douglass, eds., *To Confess the Faith Today*, 129.

9. From "A Conversation with Edward A. Dowey," by Daniel L. Migliore, *Princeton Seminary Bulletin*, new series 9, no. 2 (1988): 102. A Special Issue Honoring Edward A. Dowey. See the other outstanding essays by Janet Harbison Penfield, David Willis, Arnold B. Come, Charles C. West, C. James Trotman, and Thomas W. Gillespie. Also see "Reconciliation and Liberation—The Confession of 1967," a special issue of *Journal of Presbyterian History* 61, no. 1 (1983).

10. For an excellent summary see Eberts, *We Believe: A Study of the Book of Confessions for Church Officers, 10.*

11. John S. Conway, *The Nazi Persecution of the Churches 1933–1945* (New York: Basic Books, 1968), illustrations 9, 10.

12. Conway, *Nazi Persecution of the Churches*, p. 44n1, p. 16.

13. Additional Reading:

Victoria J. Barrett, "Transcending Barmen, Confessing in Word and Deed," *Christian Century*, May 11, 1994, 495–98.

Arthur C. Cochrane, *The Church's Confession under Hitler* (Philadelphia: Westminster Press, 1976).

Ernst Christian Helmreich, *The German Churches under Hitler: Background, Struggle and Epilogue* (Detroit: Wayne State Univ. Press, 1979).

Klaus Scholder, *A Requiem for Hitler: And Other New Perspectives on the German Church Struggle* (London: SCM Press/Philadelphia: Trinity Press, 1989).

14. John H. Leith, *Assembly at Westminster: Reformed Theology in the Making* (Richmond: John Knox Press, 1973).

15. Leith, *Assembly at Westminster*, 68.

16. Leith, *Assembly at Westminster*, 111.

17. Other objections to the Heidelberg Catechism have also been raised. In 1998 the Advocacy Committee for Women's Concerns supported the authorization of a new translation of the Heidelberg Catechism that is truthful and accurate to the original text (Overture 98-34). Since C-4.087 (Question 87) contains words not found in the German text, especially the listing of "homosexual perversion" as one of the sins that will keep sinners out of the kingdom of God, an entirely new translation was requested. The overture was not approved by the General Assembly.

18. For an excellent description of his pastorate see Harry W. Eberts, Jr., *We Believe: A Study of the Book of Confessions for Church Officers.*

19. For further reading see Shirley C. Guthrie, *Always Being Reformed: Faith for a Fragmented World* (Louisville, Ky.: Westminster John Knox Press, 1996), for a recent discussion of the struggle and development of principles of Reformed faith.

20. On October 30 and 31, 1999, Lutheran and Roman Catholic leaders gathered in Augsburg to affirm jointly that justification is no longer a doctrine that separates the two bodies of Christian faith. In this first doctrinal agreement between the Vatican and a Reformed church, both churches declare that we are saved by grace alone, and not because of any merit on our own part.

21. See John Leith, *Creeds of the Churches*, 12–19; Jack Rogers, *Presbyterian Creeds*, 62–65, discusses the final form it assumed under Charlemagne.

22. See, for example, the inspiring exposition of Karl Barth in his book *Dogmatics in Outline* (London: SCM Press, 1949, 1958).

23. *The Hymnbook* (published by the Presbyterian Church in the United States, The United Presbyterian Church in the U.S.A., and the Reformed Church in America, 1955), in "Aids To Worship," 12.

24. Leith, *Creeds of the Churches*, 29.

25. Responding to an overture from the Presbytery of Detroit, the Special Committee on the Nicene Creed was created by the 209th General Assembly in 1997 to recommend whether or not the *Book of Confessions* should be amended to include the contemporary version of the Nicene Creed rather than the traditional version. Since confessions are not merely historical documents but are used in worship, reflection, and discipline, and are living documents, the committee recommended that the substitute translation be adopted. Approved by the General Assembly in 1998, it was subsequently approved by the requisite number of presbyteries, and the change was made in the *Book of Confessions* in 1999.

26. Guthrie, *Always Being Reformed,* 21.

27. Barth, *Dogmatics in Outline*, 13.

28. *Dogmatics in Outline*, 11.

CHAPTER 7: THE ORDINATION VOWS

1. James S. Stewart, *Heralds of God*, Warrack Lectures (London: Hodder & Stoughton, 1946, 1948), 121.

2. This question was changed considerably from what it used to be. Previously it reflected the language of the Westminster Standards (C-6.002, .008, .009), "Do you believe the Scriptures of the Old and New Testaments to be the Word of God, the only infallible rule of faith and practice?" Now it is more in line with the Confession of 1967 (C-9.27). For earlier ordination questions see Cleland Boyd McAfee, *The Ruling Elder: His Duties and His Opportunities* (Philadelphia: Presbyterian Board of Christian Education, 1942), 29.

3. *Biblical Authority and Interpretation*, published by the Office of the General Assembly, PDS #70420-98-006, 1982, p. 31. This study was republished in 1998 along with *Presbyterian Understanding and Use of the Holy Scripture*, A Position Statement Adopted by the 123rd General Assembly of the Presbyterian Church

U.S. (1983). Douglas Oldenburg, Moderator of the 210th General Assembly (1998), sent both of them to all churches along with a third document, *Using the Bible: A Guided Study of Presbyterian Statements on Biblical Authority and Interpretation*, published by the Theology and Worship Ministry Unit, PDS # 277-92-101 (1993). In his letter he expresses hope that all congregations will reclaim basic Reformed principles for interpreting the Scriptures found in the *Book of Confessions* and invites every presbytery to hold a one-day conference on the subject of biblical authority for clergy and laity. Also see "Presbyterians and Biblical Authority," *Journal of Presbyterian History* 59, no. 2 (1981), which contains ten articles by various authors including David Willis, W. Eugene March, Jack Rogers, Johanna Bos, and Louis Weeks.

4. See Bradley J. Longfield, *The Presbyterian Controversy: Fundamentalists, Modernists, and Moderates* (New York/Oxford: Oxford Univ. Press, 1991); Clifton Kirkpatrick, Jr., and William H. Hopper, Jr., *What Unites Presbyterians: Common Ground for Troubled Times*), especially chapter 7, "It's in the Good Book: The Centrality of the Scriptures" (Louisville, Ky.: Geneva Press, 1997), 75–84; Jack B. Rogers and Donald K. McKim, "Pluralism and Policy in Presbyterian Views of Scripture," in *The Confessional Mosaic*, ed. Milton J Coalter, John M. Mulder, and Louis B. Weeks (Louisville, Ky.: Westminster/John Knox Press, 1990), 37–58.

5. *Biblical Authority and Interpretation*, 23.

6. *Biblical Authority and Interpretation*, 20.

7. P. T. Forsyth, *Positive Preaching and the Modern Mind*, Lyman Beecher Lectures on Preaching, Yale University, 1907 (Grand Rapids: Baker Book House, 1980) 37. Speaking of the way the Reformation rediscovered the Bible, Forsyth says, "It was not the Bible that lighted up grace for Luther, but Grace to his needy soul lighted up the Bible. Biblical preaching preaches the Gospel and uses the Bible, it does not preach the Bible and use the Gospel."

8. See Earl S. Johnson, Jr., "Biblical Authority and the Future of Biblical Preaching," *Christian Ministry*, September 1981, pp. 20–24.

9. Earl S. Johnson, Jr., "The Beatitudes for Presbyterians, Part IV, Blessed Are the Meek: Tamed by the Spirit," *Presbyterian Outlook*, September 27, 1999, p. 16.

10. Calvin, *Institutes of the Christian Religion*, 1.6.3.

11. Michael D. Bush, "The History and Meaning of *Semper Reformanda*," *Presbyterian Outlook*, September 23, 1996, 5–6. For a similar interpretation and a discussion of the history of the expression also see Harold B. Nebelsick, "Ecclesia Reformata, Semper

Reformanda," *Exploring Presbyterian Worship: Contributions from Reformed Liturgy and Music*, PDS #70430-94-001 (1994), 3–10.

12. In 1992 the General Assembly rejected Overture 96-42 from the Presbytery of Los Ranchos that proposed the affirmation of five additional tenets: the Scriptures as the infallible rule of faith and practice; the historic actuality of the virgin birth; the historic actuality of Jesus' miracles; the efficacy of substitutionary atonement; and the historic actuality of Jesus' resurrection.

13. *The Nature of the Church and the Practice of Governance*, 5–6. For further study of the Reformed tenets see *Major Themes in the Reformed Tradition*, ed. Donald K. McKim (Grand Rapids: Wm. B. Eerdmans Publishing Co., 1991). John H. Leith, *An Introduction to the Reformed Tradition* (Atlanta: John Knox Press, 1981), lists the characteristics of Reformed theology as: a theology of the holy catholic church, a theocentric theology, a theology of the Bible, predestination, the distinction between Creator and creature, theology as a practical science, and theology as practical wisdom. Also see McKim's *Basic Christian Doctrine* (Louisville, Ky.: Westminster/ John Knox Press, 1993), and Howard L. Rice, *Reformed Spirituality* (Louisville, Ky.: Westminster/John Knox Press, 1991).

14. See Longfield, *The Presbyterian Controversy*.

15. I am indebted for this understanding to Gordon I. Zimmerman, Prairie Village, Kansas, who corrected my earlier erroneous discussion of this concept in *Presbyterian Outlook* (September 4–11, 1995, 6–7) in a letter he wrote to me on January 6, 1996. For a discussion of "pure doctrine" in the Lutheran tradition, see Vergilius Ferm, "The Lutheran Church in America," in *The American Church of the Protestant Heritage*, ed. Vergilius Ferm (New York: Philosophical Library, 1953), 30, 32, 42.

16. Carol Doran and Thomas Troeger, *Open to Glory: Renewing Worship in the Congregation* (Valley Forge, Pa.: Judson Press, 1993), 78, 79, 47.

17. Archibald MacLeish, "Psyche with the Candle," *Collected Poems, 1917–1952* (Boston: Houghton Mifflin, 1952), 126.

18. Gray and Tucker, *Presbyterian Polity for Church Officers*, 16.

CHAPTER 8: ETHICAL AND PROFESSIONAL STANDARDS FOR CHURCH OFFICERS

1. Eugene Carson Blake, *Presbyterian Law for the Local Church: A Handbook for Church Officers and Members*, 63.

2. I am grateful to James S. Evinger, faculty member at the University of Rochester Medical Center, who served as chairperson

of the Investigating/Prosecution Committee, Presbytery of Genesee Valley, for calling my attention to these texts
   3. Rogers, *Presbyterian Creeds,* 92–95.
   4. Rogers, *Presbyterian Creeds,* 95.
   5. Leith, *Introduction to the Reformed Tradition,* 229–30.
   6. *Theology of Vocation,* PDS #232-91-016, p. 20. For a more detailed discussion see Walter E. Wiest and Elwyn A. Smith, *Ethics in Ministry: A Guide for the Professional* (Minneapolis: Fortress Press, 1990).

CHAPTER 9: GROWING YOUR CHURCH

   1. Alban Institute, 7315 Wisconsin Ave., Suite 1250W, Bethesda, MD 20814, phone (800) 486-1318.
   2. Available from Evangelism and Church Development, National Ministries Division (PDS #72320-95-003).
   3. Loren Mead, *The Once and Future Church: Reinventing the Congregation for a New Mission Frontier* (Washington, D.C.: Alban Institute, 1991, 1993); *Transforming Congregations for the Future* (1994). A new book by Roy Oswald and Robert Friedrich is also very useful: *Discerning Your Congregation's Future: A Strategic and Spiritual Approach* (Alban Institute, 1998). Also see Alan C. Klaas, *In Search of the Unchurched* (Alban Institute, 1989, 1996); David S. Young, *A New Heart and a New Spirit: A Plan for Renewing Your Church* (Valley Forge, Pa: Judson Press, 1994).
   4. The Synod of the Northeast, for example, arranges (for cost) to have the Percept Group, Inc. (151 Kalmus Dr., Suite A104, Costa Mesa, CA 92626–5900, phone (800) 442-6277), analyze the area in which a church is located according to parameters the church itself chooses. The resulting report is based on U.S. Census Bureau information, demographics provided by National Decision Systems, and economic data furnished by the Wharton Economic Forecasting Associates and Chase Econometrics. For ministry area demographics from the General Assembly, contact the Evangelism and Church Development Program Area, National Ministries Division, at (800) 728-7228 x5184 or x5247.
   5. Church Financial Campaign Service, 100 Witherspoon Street, Room M2002, Louisville, KY 40202–1396, phone 888–219-6513.
   6. Ignatius of Loyola, *Spiritual Exercises and Selected Works,* ed. George E. Ganss, S.J. (New York: Paulist Press, 1991), 161–65.
   7. *Spiritual Exercises,* 162.
   8. *Spiritual Exercises,* 163.

Bibliography

Angell, James W. *How to Spell Presbyterian*. Rev. ed. Philadelphia: Geneva Press, 1984.

Barrett, Victoria J. "Transcending Barmen, Confessing in Word and Deed." *Christian Century* (May 11, 1994): 495–98.

Barth, Karl. *Dogmatics in Outline*. London: SCM Press, 1949, 1958.

Beattie, Frank A. *Companion to the Constitution: Polity for Church Officers*. 4th ed. Louisville, Ky.: Geneva Press, 1996.

Beeke, Joel R., and Sinclair B. Ferguson, eds. *Reformed Confessions Harmonized: With an Annotated Bibliography of Reformed Doctrinal Works*. Grand Rapids: Baker Books, 1999.

Blake, Eugene Carson, editor. *Presbyterian Law for the Local Church: A Handbook for Church Officers and Members*. Published for the Office of the General Assembly by the Publication Division of the Board of Christian Education, 1953.

Book of Common Worship. Presbyterian Church (U.S.A.) and Cumberland Presbyterian Church. Louisville, Ky.: Westminster/John Knox Press, 1993.

Book of Order, Presbyterian Church (U.S.A.), Annotated Edition, 1999–2000. Louisville, Ky.: Presbyterian Distribution Service, 1999. #OGA-99-013.

Bush, Michael D. "The History and Meaning of *Semper Reformanda*." *Presbyterian Outlook*, September 23, 1996, pp. 5–6.

Byars, Ronald P. "Challenging the Ethos: A History of Presbyterian Worship Resources in the Twentieth Century." In *The Confessional Mosaic: Presbyterian and Twentieth Century Theology*, edited by Milton J Coalter, John M. Mulder, and Louis B. Weeks, pp. 134–61. Louisville, Ky.: Westminster/John Knox, 1990.

Calvin, John. *Institutes of the Christian Religion*. Edited by John T. McNeill, translated by Ford Lewis Battles. Philadelphia: Westminster Press, 1960.

———. *Instruction in Faith (1537)*. Translated by Paul T. Fuhrmann. Philadelphia: Westminster Press, 1949; Louisville, Ky.: Westminster/John Knox Press, 1992.

Campbell, Cynthia, and J. Frederick Holper. *Praying in Common.* Theology and Worship Occasional Paper No. 6. Keynote addresses presented at the Festivals of Worship introducing the *Book of Common Worship.* PDS #70420-94-200.

Campbell, Ted A. *Christian Confessions: A Historical Introduction.* Louisville, Ky.: Westminster John Knox Press, 1996.

Carpenter, H. J. "Minister, Ministry." In *A Theological Word Book of the Bible*, edited by Alan Richardson. New York: Macmillan Co., 1950.

Chambers, Oswald. *My Utmost for His Highest: An Updated Version in Today's Language.* Edited by James Reimann. Grand Rapids: Discovery House Publications, 1992.

Coalter, Milton J, John M. Mulder, and Louis B. Weeks, eds. *The Confessional Mosaic: Presbyterians and Twentieth-Century Theology.* Louisville, Ky.: Westminster/John Knox Press, 1990.

_____. *The Organizational Revolution: Presbyterians and American Denominationalism.* Louisville, Ky.: Westminster/John Knox Press, 1992.

_____. *The Re-Forming Tradition: Presbyterians and Mainstream Protestantism.* Louisville, Ky.: Westminster/John Knox Press, 1992.

Cochrane, Arthur C. *The Church's Confession under Hitler.* Philadelphia: Westminster Press, 1976.

_____. *Reformed Confessions of the 16th Century.* Philadelphia: Westminster Press, 1966.

Conway, John S. *The Nazi Persecution of the Churches 1933–1945.* New York: Basic Books, 1968.

Daniels, Perky. "What Presbyterians Believe: Why Do We 'Confess' Our Faith?" *Presbyterians Today*, June 1996, pp. 17–19.

Doran, Carol, and Thomas Troeger. *Open to Glory: Renewing Worship in the Congregation.* Valley Forge, Pa.: Judson Press, 2d printing, 1993.

Dowey, Edward, A., Jr. *A Commentary on the Confession of 1967 and an Introduction to The Book of Confessions.* Philadelphia: Westminster Press, 1968.

Eberts, Harry W., Jr. *We Believe: A Study of the Book of Confessions for Church Officers.* Philadelphia: Geneva Press, 1987.

Ferm, Virgilius, ed. *The American Church of the Protestant Heritage.* New York: Philosophical Library, 1953.

Forsyth, P. T. *Positive Preaching and the Modern Mind.* Lyman Beecher Lectures on Preaching, Yale University, 1907. Grand Rapids: Baker Book House, 1980.

Friedman, Edwin H. *Generation to Generation: Family Process in Church and Synagogue.* New York and London: Guilford Press, 1985.

González, Catherine Gunsalus. "The Book of Common Worship: A Theological Perspective." *Presbyterian Outlook*, September 20, 1993, p. 5.

Gray, Joan S., and Joyce C. Tucker. *Presbyterian Polity for Church Officers.* 3d ed. Louisville, Ky.: Westminster John Knox Press, 1999.

Griggs, Donald L. *In Spirit and in Truth: The Directory for Worship*. Videotape with Leader's Guide. Merchantville, N.J.: Interlink Video Productions, 1991.

Guide to Resources (1999–2000). Louisville, Ky.: Congregational Ministries Division, General Assembly Council. PDS #70358-99-001.

Guthrie, Shirley C. *Always Being Reformed: Faith for a Fragmented World*. Louisville, Ky.: Westminster John Knox Press, 1996.

Hageman, Howard G. *Pulpit and Table: Some Chapters in the History of Worship in the Reformed Churches*. Richmond: John Knox Press, 1962.

Halverstadt, Hugh F. *Managing Church Conflict*. Louisville, Ky.: Westminster/John Knox Press, 1991.

Helmreich, Ernst Christian. *The German Churches under Hitler: Background, Struggle and Epilogue*. Detroit: Wayne State University Press, 1979.

Hurlbut, Stephen A. *The Liturgy of the Church of Scotland*, part I: *Calvin's Liturgy at Strasburg and Geneva*. Washington, D.C.: St. Albans Press, 1944.

Ignatius of Loyola. *Spiritual Exercises and Selected Works*. Edited by George E. Ganss, S.J. New York: Paulist Press, 1991.

Johnson, Earl S., Jr. "The Beatitudes for Presbyterians, Part IV, Blessed Are the Meek: Tamed by the Spirit." *Presbyterian Outlook*, September 27, 1999, p. 16.

————. "Biblical Authority and the Future of Biblical Preaching." *The Christian Ministry*, September 1981, pp. 20–24.

Kirkpatrick, Clifton, Jr., and William H. Hopper, Jr. *What Unites Presbyterians: Common Ground for Troubled Times*. Louisville, Ky.: Geneva Press, 1997.

Klaas, Alan C. *In Search of the Unchurched*. Washington, D.C.: Alban Institute, 1989, 1996.

Kline, C. Benton. "The New Directory for Worship on the Use of Language." *Reformed Liturgy and Music* 23, no. 4 (1989): 190ff.

————. *A Study Guide for the Directory for Worship*. Louisville, Ky.: Presbyterian Publishing House, 1990.

Leith, John H. *Assembly at Westminster: Reformed Theology in the Making*. Richmond: John Knox Press, 1973.

————. *Basic Christian Doctrine*. Louisville, Ky.: Westminster/John Knox Press, 1993.

————. *Creeds of the Churches: A Reader in Christian Doctrine from the Bible to the Present*. New York: Doubleday & Co., Anchor Books, 1963.

————. *An Introduction to the Reformed Tradition: A Way of Being the Christian Community*. Rev. ed. Atlanta: John Knox Press, 1981.

Longfield, Bradley J. *The Presbyterian Controversy: Fundamentalists, Modernists, and Moderates*. New York and Oxford: Oxford University Press, 1991.

MacLeish, Archibald. "Psyche With the Candle." *Collected Poems, 1917–1952*, 126. Boston: Houghton Mifflin, 1952.

Manual, for Church Officers and Members, of the Government, Discipline, and Worship of the Presbyterian Church in the United States of America. 16th ed. Philadelphia: Office of the General Assembly, 1950.

Martin, Clarice. "Inclusive Language and the Brief Statement of Faith: Widening the Margins in Our Common Confession." In *To Confess the Faith Today*, edited by Jack L. Stotts and Jane Dempsey Douglass, 107–29. Louisville, Ky.: Westminster/John Knox Press, 1990.

Maxwell, William D. *A History of Worship in the Church of Scotland.* London: Oxford University Press, 1955.

McAfee, Cleland Boyd. *The Ruling Elder: His Duties and His Opportunities.* Philadelphia: Presbyterian Board of Christian Education, 1942.

McCarthy, David B. "The Emerging Importance of Presbyterian Polity." In *The Organizational Revolution, Presbyterians and American Denominationalism.* Edited by Milton J Coalter, John M. Mulder, and Louis B. Weeks. Louisville, Ky.: Westminster/John Knox Press, 1992, pp. 279–306.

McKim, Donald, ed. *Major Themes in the Reformed Tradition.* Grand Rapids: Wm. B. Eerdmans Publishing Co., 1992.

McKim, LindaJo H. *The Presbyterian Hymnal Companion.* Louisville, Ky.: Westminster/John Knox Press, 1993.

Mead, Loren. *The Once and Future Church: Reinventing the Congregation for a New Mission Frontier.* Washington, D.C.: Alban Institute, 1991, 1993.

_____. *Transforming Congregations for the Future.* Washington, D.C.: Alban Institute, 1994.

Meister, J. W. Greg. *To All Generations: The Book of Confessions.* Videotape. Merchantville, N.J.: Interlink Video Productions, n.d.

Migliore, Daniel L. "A Conversation with Edward A. Dowey," *Princeton Seminary Bulletin*, n.s., 9, no. 2 (1988): 89–103. A Special Issue Honoring Edward A. Dowey.

Miller, Herb. "When Should I Say Goodbye?" *Net Results*, April 1996, pp. 4–13.

The Nature of the Church and the Practice of Governance. Approved by the 205th General Assembly (1993) of the Presbyterian Church (U.S.A.). Published by the Office of the General Assembly, 1993.

Nebelsick, Harold B. "Ecclesia Reformata, Semper Reformanda." *Exploring Presbyterian Worship: Contributions from Reformed Liturgy and Music*, 1994, pp. 3–10. PDS #70430-94-001.

Old, Hughes Oliphant. *Worship That Is Reformed according to Scriptures.* Guides to the Reformed Tradition. Edited by John H. Leith and John W. Kuykendall. Atlanta: John Knox Press, 1984.

Oswald, Roy. *Running through the Thistles: Terminating a Ministerial Relationship with a Parish.* Washington, D.C.: Alban Institute, 1978.

Oswald, Roy, and Robert Friedrich. *Discerning Your Congregation's Future, A Strategic and Spiritual Approach.* Washington, D.C.: Alban Institute, 1998.

Pastoral Expectations Inventory. New York: United Presbyterian Church in the U.S.A., 1976.

Pfleiderer, David Hoyt. "Are We Getting Too Much Ritual in Our Presbyterian Worship?" *Presbyterian Outlook*, August 2–9, 1993, p. 8.

Phillips, Timothy R., and Dennis L. Okholm, editors. *The Nature of Confession: Evangelicals and Postliberals in Conversation.* Downers Grove, Ill.: InterVarsity Press, 1996.

Presbyterians and Biblical Authority. Special issue of *Journal of Presbyterian History* 59, no. 2 (1981).

Reconciliation and Liberation: The Confession of 1967. Special issue of *Journal of Presbyterian History* 61 (spring 1983).

Rice, Howard L. *Reformed Spirituality: An Introduction for Believers.* Louisville, Ky.: Westminster/John Knox Press, 1991.

Rogers, Jack. "Essential Tenets of the Reformed Faith," and "Touring the Creeds." Videotape. Arroyo Grande, Calif.: Essential Media Services.

———. "Introduction to A New Brief Statement of Faith." Videotape. Arroyo Grande, Calif.: Essential Media Services.

———. *Presbyterian Creeds: A Guide to the Book of Confessions.* Philadelphia: Westminster John Knox Press, 1985, 1991.

Rogers, Jack B., and Donald K. McKim. "Pluralism and Policy in Presbyterian Views of Scripture." In *The Confessional Mosaic: Presbyterians and Twentieth-Century Theology*, edited by Milton J Coalter, John M. Mulder, and Louis B. Weeks, 37–58. Louisville, Ky.: Westminster/John Knox Press, 1990.

Rohls, Jan. *Reformed Confessions: Theology from Zurich to Barmen.* Louisville, Ky.: Westminster John Knox Press, 1998.

Schillebeeckx, Edward. *Ministry: Leadership in the Community of Jesus Christ.* New York: Crossroad, 1981.

Scholder, Klaus. *A Requiem for Hitler: And Other New Perspectives on the German Church Struggle.* London: SCM Press/Philadelphia: Trinity Press, 1989.

Smith, William S. *Hymnsearch: Indexes for The Presbyterian Hymnal*, 1995. Address inquiries to the author, 1826 Ridgeover Place, Jackson, MS 39211.

So What Is God Up to in Your World and Mine? A Resource Book for Leaders Doing Training in Congregational Development. Louisville, Ky.: Evangelism and Church Development, National Ministries Division. PDS #72320-95-003.

Stake, Donald Wilson. *The ABCs of Worship: A Concise Dictionary.* Louisville. Ky.: Westminster/John Knox Press, 1992.

———. "The Book of Common Worship 1993." *Presbyterian Outlook*, September 6, 1993, p. 6.

Stewart, James S. *Heralds of God.* Warrack Lectures. London: Hodder & Stoughton/New York: Charles Scribner's Sons, 1946, 1948.

Stotts, Jack L., and Jane Dempsey Douglass. *To Confess the Faith Today.* Louisville, Ky.: Westminster/John Knox Press, 1990.

Thompson, Bard. *Liturgies of the Western Church.* Cleveland: Meridian Books, 1961.

Through Jesus Christ: Worship and Faith. Videotape. Presbyterian Distribution Service. PDS #076908.

Trefz, Edward. *Nominating Church Officers.* Revised by W. Ben Lane. PDS #060001.

Using the Bible: A Guided Study of Presbyterian Statements on Biblical Authority and Interpretation. Louisville, Ky.: Theology and Ministry Unit, 1993. PDS #277-92-101.

Venable, William H. *Your Job as a Church Officer: A Manual for Officers of the Local Presbyterian (USA) Congregation.* Pittsburgh: Rivertree Christian Ministries, 12th printing, 1998.

Weatherhead, Leslie D. *A Private House of Prayer.* Nashville: Abingdon Press, 1958, 1979.

Wessler, Daniel P. "Why a New Directory Now?" *Reformed Liturgy and Music*, 23, no. 4 (1989): 174 .

White, Edward, A. *Saying Goodbye: A Time of Growth for Congregations and Pastors.* Washington, D.C.: Alban Institute, 1990.

Wiest, Walter E., and Elwyn A. Smith. *Ethics in Ministry: A Guide for the Professional.* Minneapolis: Fortress Press, 1990.

Wilkins, Lewis, L. "The American Presbytery in the Twentieth Century." In *The Organization Revolution: Presbyterian and American Denominationalism*, ed. Milton J Coalter, John M. Mulder, and Louis B. Weeks, pp. 96–121. Louisville, Ky.: Westminster/John Knox Press, 1992.

Witherspoon, Eugene D., Jr., and Marvin Simmers, editors. *Called to Serve: A Workbook for Training Nominating Committees and Church Officers.* Louisville, Ky.: Curriculum Publishing, Presbyterian Church (U.S.A.), 1997.

Young, David S. *A New Heart and a New Spirit: A Plan for Renewing Your Church.* Valley Forge, Pa.: Judson Press, 1994.

Index of Scripture References

/ 191

Index of *Book of Order* References

General Index

apostles, 2, 5, 6, 9, 10, 80, 111, 146–47
appeals, 46, 84, 90
ardor (and order), 42, 136

baptism, 41, 60, 65–69, 74
Barth, Karl, 100–101, 116–17, 181 n.22
Bible, 1, 23, 96, 135
  authority and interpretation, 56, 96, 99, 101, 105, 109, 114, 117, 120–24, 132, 135, 145, 153–54, 182 n.7
  and "rule of love," 110
  study of, 23, 33, 64–65, 257
  and vows of church officers, 141–43
bishop, in New Testament, 7, 8, 10, 131, 142, 144
Blake, Eugene Carson, 45, 84, 142
Book of Common Worship, 50–55, 67
Book of Confessions, 94–117, 148
  Apostles' Creed, 111, 112
  Brief Statement of Faith, A, 97
  Confession of 1967, 95, 98–101, 103, 114, 120–22, 131, 135, 150, 153, 181 n.2

Heidelberg Catechism, 95, 106–8, 148, 180 n.4
  Nicene Creed, 112, 113, 181 n.25
  Scots Confession, 95, 106, 109–11, 124, 133, 148
  Second Helvetic Confession, 42, 95, 107, 108, 149
  Theological Declaration of Barmen, 101–3
  Westminster Confession, 40, 50, 65, 98, 99, 100, 103–6, 133, 143, 148–49, 181 n.2
call to ministry, 1–5, 14–20, 23, 26, 50–54, 82, 98, 100–103, 126, 127, 129–30, 134–39, 142, 145, 150–55, 163
Calvin, John, 40, 50, 65, 70, 71, 81, 82, 95, 99, 106–7, 110, 124
censure, 89
Christian educators, 33, 34
church growth, 29, 30, 156–62
clerk of session, 35–36, 79, 90
complaints, 46, 84, 90, 92
conflict in the church, 17, 36, 77–93, 111, 132, 147
congregation
  meetings of, 4
  nominating process, 3–4, 12, 24–28